Prais

Whispers of

G000150428

Ajayan's book, *Whispers of the Himalaya*, is an incredible story that reveals the truth we are all capable of finding when we quiet our minds. I have been there in my life due to a near death and past-life experience, and as I read his story, I could feel it all happening to me. Read this book, let yourself be touched by his words and his journey as I was, and know that we all have that potential within us. Quieting my mind has been my hardest lesson, but we can all find our cave, because with faith, the rock of ages will cleft for thee...

— Bernie Siegel, MD, author of *A Book of Miracles* and *365 Prescriptions For The Soul*

Ajayan's *Whispers of the Himalaya* is an engrossing, powerful read. I picked it up one evening and stayed with it to the end, feeling as if I was with Ajayan on his journey into the spiritual heart of India and humanity. While some of us might dream of retreating from the world and living in a cave in the Himalayas near the sacred Ganges River, Ajayan shows us what that experience would actually be like, both the sublime and the mundane. He writes from the depth of the wisdom and stillness he experienced; this book is not only a memoir, but also a spiritual transmission.

— HeatherAsh Amara, author of *Warrior Goddess Training*

This book is profound! For a baby-boomer longing to touch the hem of the garment, this is just what I needed to read. Ajayan Borys gently reminds us that even in the quest to find more of ourselves, there is a balance in recognizing that we are always exactly where we are supposed to be, reinforcing the knowledge and belief that our life is unfolding in perfect harmony every single moment. He compassionately uses personal experience and revelation to lead readers out of the dream-world illusion of achievement and into a mindset that is in harmony with what is, with *Being*.

— Debra Meehl, President / Founder of The Meehl Foundation, nationally recognized speaker, Life Coach, Coauthor of *Joyful Transformation*

Loved it! Deeply moving and inspiring journey to the source. A must read for all seekers of the truth.

— Michael Mastro, author of *The Way of Vastu*

Ajayan Borys is one of America's most experienced teachers of meditation and after many years he has released *Whispers of the Himalaya*, a biographical account of his youthful experience while living in a cave for a two-month meditation sadhana in the Himalayas. This is a very readable diary written with an exquisite composition of prose and prosody.

His weaving of the experience is skillfully constructed, with sincerity and compassion, and we, as readers, cannot avoid confronting the dilemmas of such a serious sadhana. Thus we face our own internal struggle with the mind versus a monumental aspiration that takes place with those seeking an inner path.

I have not encountered such a forthright account by a Westerner of what is entailed in such a situation. The Ego and the Ideal become pitted against each other, and we cannot avoid the conflicting tales our Ego tells us to keep us comfortable in an illusion versus the reality we imagine we seek.

His story is our story, and the reader will emerge a better, more cleansed, more realistic human, and hopefully shed many mental constructs that do not serve, other than to preserve our false personae.

Highly recommended for all on the road seeking to move from the "human" to the "humane" and beyond.

— Swami Anandakapila Saraswati 2017, author of *A Chakra and Kundalini Workbook*, and *Ecstasy Through Tantra*

Ajayan sharing his experiences in the Himalayas is beautiful, insightful, inspirational, and entertaining. His wit regarding his experiences as well as the challenges he faced provide an enjoyable story, while offering astute observations of the path toward enlightenment. I recommend this book to anyone interested in the journey of meditation and higher consciousness.

— Kerry McClure, BS, RYT, NC, BCHN®, Co-author of *Beyond Meditation: Making Mindfulness Accessible for Everyone*

A wonderful and engaging description of a personal pilgrimage towards enlightenment. In *Whispers of the Himalaya* Ajayan Borys evocatively brings forth the memories of people, places, and personal growth. With gentle, flowing language he shares his search for spiritual divine connection. Frankly honest and with unwavering self-reflection, he shares the deep reflections of a journey of a lifetime, interweaving his experiences with insights and spiritual expressions that keep you coming back to them to re-read again and again. This book is so well written, you feel you are there with him.

— Mira Dessy, BCHHP, Co-author of *Beyond Meditation: Making Mindfulness Accessible for Everyone*

Whispers of the
Himalaya

AJAYAN BORYS

purna
press

purna
press

119 Skylark Lane
Friday Harbor, Washington 98250

The events in this book are true and took place in the summer of 1996. In a few cases, minor details have been changed to protect the identities of the individuals involved.

Library of Congress Control Number: 2017946861

First printing, November 2017
ISBN 978-1-878041-02-9

Cover art and illustrations by Goce Ilievski.

Ordering Information
Special discounts are available on quantity purchases by corporations, associations, educators, and others. For details contact the publisher at info@purnapress.com.

Booking, Press, and Speaking Inquiries
Ajayan leads meditation retreats in North America, the Himalayas, and Peru. For information on his retreats or to book him for an interview or as a speaker, contact ajayan@ajayan.com. For information on his online and live courses, see www.ajayan.com or contact him at ajayan@ajayan.com.

Dedication

For those with the lure of the Infinite in their hearts.

Contents

Introduction

Looking back over my 65 years on this planet, I see a few unmistakable spiritual turning points in my life. One of the most memorable took place in the spring and summer of 1996. For two months, I lived at 10,000 feet in the Himalayas near the source of the Ganges River—in a cave, alone and in silence—meditating. Though that may sound dreadfully boring, as it turned out, it was the inner and outer adventure of a lifetime, and it tested and instructed me in ways I could not have imagined. This book is the account of those two months.

Just prior to that Himalayan retreat, I was living in Kerala in the far south of India, in the ashram of Mata Amritanandamayi (Ammachi). My wife, two daughters, and I had moved there a couple of years before. I was serving as the meditation teacher there. One day, a friend told me about a holy place in the Himalayas near the source of the Ganges River. He had visited there the previous year and described its incredible beauty with enthusiasm; surrounded by snow-capped peaks and remote, it was the "perfect place to meditate." He knew well my passion for meditation and my yearning for a retreat after two years of busy, noisy ashram life.

His description sounded good. Very good. But I wrestled with the thought of leaving my family. My daughters were only 8 and 15 years old. Would they feel deserted by their dad? For sure, I would not go without my family's blessing. To my surprise, both my wife and daughters generously agreed that I should go (they also know me well). So with their blessings, I traveled the entire length of India, from the far south to its northern border high in the Himalayas, and my retreat began . . .

To help you really understand my motivation for this solitary Himalayan sojourn, I would like to take you back much further, to the first spiritual turning point of my life. This took place when I was 18 years old. It radically altered my spiritual compass and set my life on a unique course that persists to this day. Ultimately, it is the reason I was living in India and why I went to the Himalayas.

Recounting this experience, I squirm more than a little. The reckless antics of my youth are not something I am proud of. I'd rather my friends and I hadn't been so willing to subject our bodies and psyches to entirely unknown, but hopefully beneficent chemistry. Be that as it may, this particular experience was pivotal—the spiritual and psychic atom bomb required to open me to the spiritual path.

It was 1970, and this Friday night, like many others, I sat in the back seat of a car with four close friends at the local teenage hangout. Yes, to complete the cliché, it was even a hamburger joint. Several hours before, we had each partaken of a psychedelic drug that my best friend had loosely referred to as mescaline.

My friends and I were talking excitedly. It is impossible to say exactly what we talked about, but perhaps more important than what we said was the experience we shared in saying it. We were of one mind; before anyone could finish a thought, another would chime in to affirm an idea, or take the thought a step further towards what seemed profound truth. It was a *superfluid* conversation. Indeed, I believe it was this very phenomenon that was the subject of our conversation—how we were of one mind and one heart, for as we shared, a miraculous unity of love and joy bonded us. To feel this, note it, and communicate it, only made it stronger. In exploring this unity of love and joy, we knew we were exploring a higher state of being, a state of greater truth, one unmistakably closer to the source and meaning of our human existence.

As we continued talking, our conversation became ever more profound and frictionless. We hardly had to say a word and unfathomable truths were communicated, and the unity of love and ecstatic joy deepened. At one point, something changed; my thinking dipped into an entirely new level, such that I could no longer speak my thoughts aloud. I had no idea what was happening to me. It seemed my thoughts were too all-encompassing and too profound to be expressed in words, and at the same time, I was overcome with a degree of love and sheer ecstasy that could not be described. That love and bliss was universal in dimension, sublime, near the very heart of creation.

My thoughts came faster and faster and with laser-like intensity. I continued to traverse deeper into finer realms of truth. Then I felt another distinct shift: No longer was I thinking in language at all. My "thoughts" were now abstract currents, powerful streams of pure intelligence and energy, so much more potent, so much more profound than language could ever convey. I was no longer thinking *about* anything; thought—pure flowing energy and intelligence, the substance and essence of life itself—*was* my focus.

By this point, I had lost all awareness of the external world. I had no awareness of where I was or whether my eyes were open or closed. I was immersed in abstract flows of pure intelligence, becoming more and more powerful each moment, flowing faster and faster, revolving around an invisible core. As those streams of pure intelligence whirled around this core, I knew I was onto the very secret of the universe. Ecstasy and love filled me. More and more profound truth, more love, more bliss—intense, indescribable—and then . . . I touched that Core.

For a timeless, eternal moment, I was not. There was no car, no parking lot, no friends, no world, no universe, no me, not an atom of existence, nothing. Yet I would be left with an indelible impression of what I had dissolved into, and it was not mere nothingness. Far from it.

I will try to convey that Core by way of metaphor. Imagine you are the sun—incomprehensibly vast, immeasurable energy and light. Think of it: the sun is so huge that its mass alone accounts for 99.86% of all mass in our solar system. It is a body of inestimable energy, a minuscule fraction of which supplies nearly all of the energy that supports life here on Earth. So again, imagine you *are* that incomprehensible mass of light and heat, the sun. Only instead of qualities of heat, energy, and light, you are a vast mass of light, energy, love, bliss, and pure intelligence. Nonetheless, as vast as you are (as the sun is), somewhere you end; there is an edge, an end to your being.

So, imagine you are a billion suns, or even a billion trillion suns—of pure light, energy, love, bliss, and intelligence. No one can really imagine what that would mean. How huge would that mass be? How much intelligence, energy, and love? Still, somewhere you would end.

Well, what I dissolved into was this, only without end—an absolute, infinite ocean of light, energy, love, bliss, and pure intelligence, without limit. Yet across the entire expanse of that infinite ocean, there was not the slightest stir of activity, not a single wave or impulse whatsoever, not so much as an atom rousing. It was absolute, perfect Peace.

To complete this picture, I must add I had the distinct impression of that Infinitude as somehow spherical in nature, only a sphere without end, without edge, without shape, thus not a sphere at all, but rather perfect, infinite wholeness, absolutely complete as well as unbounded.

I do not know how long I disappeared into that state, for there was no time there, but when I finally did reappear, my eyes, I found, were open. I was still sitting with my friends in the back seat of the car.

"That . . .was . . .God . . ." I whispered in awe.

Prior to this dissolving, I would have certainly said that I believed in God, but now it was no longer a matter of belief. From that eternal moment, I *knew* God. (Devoid of every bit of meaning, association, connotation, image, or idea of what that word means. I knew the Reality, infinitely beyond words or ideas. So if that word holds a charge for you, please bear with me for the moment without judging it.) When you dissolve into the Infinite, there can be no mistake. There is no room for doubt or question, and your certainty is not a matter of dogma or doctrine, but of direct experience.*

Prior to my falling away from our conversation, my friends and I had been perfectly united, so I assumed they had all experienced what I just had. I fully expected them

---

* Actually, not exactly true: when you merge with the Infinite, it is not an *experience*. There is no you left to experience and no object to experience. There is just Infinity. Only afterwards, when you emerge from That, do you feel you had an experience. This residual impression of the Infinite was far more impactful on my life than any other experience I've had.

to concur with an awe equivalent to my own. Instead, they looked at me with puzzled expressions.

Seeing the looks on their faces, I persisted. "Didn't you . . . experience It?" I asked. "The Light? God?"

They just looked at me. A big, unspoken, unanimous, "Huh?" hung in the car.

The rest of that night, while my friends continued their conversation, and later, while they slept in my best friend's basement, I stayed wide awake privately assimilating what had happened to me, what I was still filled to the brim with, for that Infinity had left Its mark in my being.

In fact, this was remarkable: I now knew things I had never known before. Dissolving into Infinity had imprinted me with several self-evident truths.

- I knew with utter certainty anyone could attain union with That, and abide in that Infinitude for all eternity. In fact, I knew That, the Infinite, was the final goal of all existence.*
- Though I had dissolved into Infinity with the help of a drug, the drug was incidental. That I had taken

---

* Over the years, I have met a number of people who expressed fear of losing their individuality in merging with the Infinite. I admit, intellectually the prospect is daunting. Who wants to completely disappear? But having experienced that dissolving, I can say there is no need for fear at all. Indeed, merging into Infinitude is fulfilling far beyond any conception of the highest heaven. There is simply no comparison. Our ideas of heaven are not even a shadow of That. Besides, as I subsequently learned, enlightenment does not mean you are dissolved and gone for good. You can still operate in the world; you have simply realized your true identity as one with the universal Self.

a drug did not invalidate the experience. No drug could fabricate Infinity. No drug could generate God. The finite does not give rise to the Infinite, but somehow, the drug had opened me to that ultimate state.

- To achieve that final Goal of existence—eternal union with the Divine—to experience more than just a glimpse, required much more than a drug could provide. In fact, it required just the opposite: an extraordinary degree of purity and what I thought of as "normalcy." How could one achieve that infinite intelligence, light, bliss, and love, without purity of being? How could one achieve That without becoming normal in the highest sense of the word—whole, natural, pure, simple, innocent, having straightened any and all crooked places in one's heart and mind? The moment I emerged from that state, I knew I would never take recreational drugs again. I would give up all the vices my friends and I had taken to: smoking, drinking, as well as drugs. A drug may have allowed me to dissolve into the Infinite, but now I had to leave that catalyst behind for good.

So began my spiritual path. Initially, it was not an easy one. My deepest friendships quickly became a source of extreme dissonance. Over the next few weeks, I would try over and over to persuade my friends, especially my best friend, to stop taking drugs, stop drinking, and stop smoking, so they could join me in striving for that state of normalcy, but they simply could not relate. No one could.

I began to feel isolated. I looked around at my friends and saw a glaring contradiction that I could not understand. Deep within, they knew their drinking, smoking, and getting high was not good for them; so why did they do these things? Yes, I had done these same things, even though I knew they weren't good for me. So I should have understood their sense of adventure and invulnerability to any possible danger. But now it seemed so clearly wrong to me. Why lie to yourself at the risk of damaging your life? In fact, we already had one friend living in a mental institution from drug use, and we'd had numerous near accidents driving under the influence. What were we doing? But ultimately, my efforts to persuade my friends were futile. They saw me as the strange one, and so I soon drifted away from them.

In the weeks and months following my experience, I saw this same disturbing pattern of rationalization not just in my teenage friends, but wherever I looked. Why did nearly everyone rationalize behavior they knew was not true? Why, for instance, did my parents argue? Did they not also know better? Couldn't they graciously come to an understanding without yelling? Why did anyone become angry with anyone else? Why did my sister talk on the phone for hours while her homework went undone? Why was our society rationalizing the war in Vietnam? Why was there even such a thing as war in the first place?

One could say all this is just human nature, but that, it now seemed to me, was a meaningless excuse. Surely it is within our power to NOT act those ways. So why do we do it? I began to feel that I was living in a bizarre world in which self-deception and acting against what was self-evidently true or simply honest was the acceptable norm—which meant I was the crazy one.

It was as if the experience of the Infinite had made a level of mind that was subconscious for most now conscious for me—and this was disturbing because of the contradictions it revealed. I began to feel I was crazy, that living sensibly and with integrity—what seemed to me the obvious way to live—was consciously rejected by everyone to one degree or another, but without any rational reason for that rejection. It was simply universally accepted, unthinkingly, and this began to cause me no end of anxiety. Surely not everyone could be wrong. What was wrong with me?

Then one day, I spotted a little book with a strange name on my father's bookcase. I do not know what drew me to it, but I picked it up. The title was *The Bhagavad-Gita*, with an introduction by Aldous Huxley.

I was captivated as I skimmed through its pages. I had never seen this book before, but I knew it intimately. I knew it so well, it was as if I had written it myself. Its descriptions of the Atman* and Brahman† perfectly described my own experience of the Infinite. I knew with certainty what the author was referring to with phrases like "Being of beings, Changeless, eternal," and "bliss in the eternal." There was no doubt the author of this book knew well the Infinitude I had dissolved into when he wrote:

He is all-knowing God, lord of the emperors,
Ageless, subtler far than mind's inmost subtlety,
Universal sustainer,
Shining sunlike, self-luminous.‡

---

*   The infinite, higher Self within the individual.

†   The great homogeneous wholeness of the infinite Self, within which all the objects of the universe and all of time and space are insubstantial superimpositions.

‡   Swami Prabhavananda and Isherwood, Christopher, trans. *The Song of God: Bhagavad-Gita*. New York, New York: The New American Library, Inc., 1951: 75.

The realization that my experience was not entirely unique, that there were others who had known that same Infinitude, brought inexpressible relief and excitement. After skimming the book, I tried to meditate—something I had never conceived of doing before—but my efforts were unsuccessful. Yet the experience in the car had given me something. Sitting in my bedroom, I could feel an inner spiritual energy. It sometimes seemed this power was sufficient for me to levitate for instance, or to read minds. But not knowing how to direct that power, not having any idea of what to do with it, I sat at a loss.

I began to seek out other spiritual books and somehow discovered *The Tibetan Book of the Great Liberation: Or the Method of Realizing Nirvana through Knowing the Mind,* edited by W. Y. Evans-Wentz. Again, reading of the "One Mind," "All Consciousness," "Clear Light," and "enlightenment" resonated with my own experience. I decided that I had to travel to Tibet, find a master, and seek enlightenment.

There were a few problems with this plan, however. I was still in high school and scheduled to start college the following year. To depart from this course would create major conflict with my parents. Besides, I had no money to get to Tibet. Even if I had the money, I probably couldn't get into the country, as it was still in chaos from Chinese occupation.

The next fall I enrolled in college, and when one day I saw a poster for a course in meditation, I decided to investigate. At the introductory lecture, the teacher in blue suit and red tie was a turnoff for me, and nothing he said about developing "full creative potential" and "perfect health" really struck home. But he did say one thing that piqued my interest: "the field of inner Being is a field of *absolute stability.*"

I was still suffering from anxiety and feeling unstable and stressed from my lonely sojourn into spirituality. My mind was not normal in another way, too: I kept having vivid flashes of being in ancient Greece. These flashes came on unexpectedly. I would feel the entire ambiance of Hellenic society and the Greek countryside, as if I were really there. These may have actually been flashes of a past life, but they were extremely disconcerting at the time.

I had also read a book on Tibetan Buddhism by Alexandra David-Neel, and her descriptions of the psychological torments of monks lacking the requisite balance and stability had concerned me. I knew I would have to be far more stable than I was at that point to successfully tread the path of Tibet's more esoteric teachings. Perhaps this beginner's technique of meditation would help prepare me. I signed up.

On the final day of the course, our teacher let his hair down and began talking of something that actually interested me: cosmic consciousness, Self-realization. After the session, I went up to him.

"This is it, isn't it?" I asked him. "This is the pure, clear light, the infinite Absolute."

He smiled and nodded, and I was hooked. Perhaps I wouldn't have to go to Tibet after all. Meditating 20 minutes twice a day was purportedly all that was required for enlightenment.

In the first few months of meditating, my anxiety and instability was soothed and healed. Before long, I was drawn to traveling the world to study with the founder of this method of meditation, Maharishi Mahesh Yogi. I became a teacher of his techniques (the Transcendental Meditation® program), spent many months at a time meditating for not 40 minutes a day, but 8 to 12 hours a day, and received countless ecstatic spiritual experiences. For over a decade, I taught the Transcendental Meditation® program.

In those years, I experienced many hours of dwelling in a state distinctly similar to what I'd glimpsed in the back seat of that car. I had not been disappointed. What I learned from Maharishi was invaluable, and the time I spent with him a great blessing, but clearly, even years later, I was still yearning for full-time natural abidance in the infinite Self, enlightenment.

Then, in 1988 I met Ammachi, a remarkable embodiment of pure, divine love. My family and I grew close with her over the next few years; she stayed with us when she visited Seattle. Eventually, we were drawn to living with her at her ashram in Kerala. While encouraging my dedication to meditation, even generously assigning me the post of meditation teacher at her ashram, she emphasized the critical outward expression of spirituality in terms of love, compassion, and selfless service. It is an emphasis I have grown to appreciate more and more, even to this day.

That is, in short, the back story of my Himalayan retreat. Why would I even think of going to the Himalayas to meditate for weeks or months? Hopefully the answer to that is now obvious. It was a rare opportunity. Who knows what could be achieved with full dedication to the Goal? Discovering the answer to that question inspired me to travel some 1700 miles, find a cave at 10,000 feet in a remote forest near the source of the Ganga,* close my eyes, and embark on the adventure of a lifetime.

---

*   The Ganges River.

CHAPTER 1

The Source

I awoke to a roaring noise. It filled my room as if I was
bunking with a locomotive. *What could make such a
sound,* I wondered. I had no idea. Then I realized: It was
the Ganga rushing by, only 100 feet from my room in the
tattered ashram I'd found the night before. I had been so
exhausted from over 100 hours of travel by train and bus
from India's southern tip, I hadn't even noticed the river.

I am in Gangotri, the source of the Ganga. I have made it!

It was not yet 5 a.m. I threw on some clothes,
wrapped myself in my meditation shawl, and stepped
out into the courtyard, which in the moonlight, I now
saw was lush with flowering gardens. The air at 10,000
feet was clear and cold, and huge cliffs and snow-capped
peaks towered around me. But it was the river, rushing by
in its power, that attracted my attention.

At lower elevations, in Rishikesh, the Ganga had been
several hundred yards wide, flowing languidly, like a vast
expanse of milk chocolate. Here, in Gangotri, it could not

have been more than 70 feet across, but it was a gushing torrent of pure, unbridled energy. Its whitish waters rose in turbulent waves, rushing with astonishing speed, threatening to leap over its banks at any moment. Watching the river in that soft light of the moon was mesmerizing. Lured by its power, I descended some steps to its bank and made my way onto a large white boulder jutting into the water. I laid down a small cotton carpet and sat to meditate.

To my amazement, almost instantly I was in another world. My body sat beside the Ganga, but my mind was in heaven. There is a saying in India that everywhere in this world is the earth, but the Himalaya is heaven. In that moment, it seemed to me not just a saying. Despite the past five days of grueling travel, my mind now floated effortlessly in a blissful realm of golden, celestial light. The exquisite presence of the Divine thrilled my heart. *Such a sublime meditation can only be due to the holiness of this place . . .*

Over an hour passed before I again felt myself on the earth. The river carried the coolness of melting glaciers, and an icy breeze washed over me. I was really here, in the Himalayas, just a stone's throw from Tibet.

Stars still shone in the clear, deep blue sky. Yet the hint of dawn revealed dark cliffs rising straight up for a thousand feet or more on either side of the village. Silhouettes of rugged, snow-capped peaks adorned the high end of the valley, beyond which were the first rays of light. Opposite this, the lower end of the valley opened to an endless range of shadowy mountain peaks. A white stone temple stood directly across the river from me. For a few minutes, I surveyed the scene, filled with peace and calm. Then I noticed a few Indian pilgrims approaching the Ganga for their morning bath, and I realized, *I hadn't yet bathed in that holy river!*

Somehow this seemed urgent. To bathe in the holy Ganga is said to be a great blessing that purifies the devout of all their sins. Having traveled the length of India to get here, I saw no reason to delay. I certainly had plenty of accumulated sins to purify.

I crossed a metal foot bridge over the river to the bathing ghat* adjacent to the Gangotri temple. Here the river's flow was broken by some boulders, providing a spot where I could walk into the water without being washed away.

A few more male Indian pilgrims were beginning their morning bath at the ghat, gingerly negotiating rocks and boulders in their bare feet, dressed only in their underpants. They used plastic cups to pour the icy water over themselves, then dashed back to their towels and quickly dried and dressed in the frigid air. I hadn't thought to bring a cup. I would have to dunk.

I undressed to my underpants, fully exposed to the cold. Though Indians are modest as a rule, this state of undress was entirely acceptable (for men) under the circumstances. In fact, it was expected at a bathing ghat such as this. Women were expected to bathe either in a long swim dress, or while wearing a sari. However, no women were present.

I walked clumsily on the freezing rocks a few feet out into the river, which was swift and powerful. The air was so cold my breath made clouds of steam, but the water was far colder yet—liquid ice. After taking a few steps into that icy flow, my feet were completely numbed.

Mentally bracing myself, I sat in the water, spasmed with shivers, then lay on my back in a shallow pool protected from the rapids by boulders. Just for an instant I

---

*   Stairs leading to a holy river to facilitate bathing.

allowed my body and head to dip completely under. *God!!!* It was almost unbearable. My mind itself seemed to freeze.

I leapt to my feet, collected myself, and dunked again, holding my breath while the freezing flow rushed over me. When I emerged, my brain felt like an ice cube. I could only trust I had not permanently damaged myself.

By this time, all the Indian men present were watching me, their cups held limply in their hands. Apparently, I was the only one who literally "bathed" in the freezing Ganga at that altitude. I did my best to give no outward indication of any discomfort. Hey, didn't everyone do this? We all did in America . . . Only vaguely did I realize how caught I was in my attachment to looking good, an attachment that would, before my trip ended, be annihilated.

Returning to the river's bank, dripping and exultant, I stood atop a large, white boulder. I had taken my first bath in the Ganga at Gangotri, the river's very source—a full immersion, too. I reveled in the sense of having undergone an initiation into something mysteriously close to the heart of India. Now, perhaps, I would be graced to find a cave and begin my retreat.

*And I just **have** to get one of those bathing cups.*

CHAPTER 2
Search for a Cave

As I approached Krishnashram, where I was staying, I saw a few Indian pilgrims and Western tourists waiting for breakfast. The Swami who had greeted me upon my arrival the night before stooped out from one of the huts and came in my direction. He was wrapped in a tattered orange wool shawl, and despite his long, disheveled hair and unkempt beard, he was a handsome fellow. He appeared to be in his late thirties.

"Hari Om!" he called out, smiling broadly, the palms of his hands joined and raised high in greeting. His eyes were opened unnaturally wide, and this with his toothy smile gave him a wild, crazed look; but at least he seemed friendly.

"Om Namah Shivayah," I said. This was the standard greeting I'd learned while living in Kerala. Like "Hari Om," it is a mantra that honors the divine spark in the other person, far preferable to a simple "hello"—among spiritual folk anyway. By using such greetings, every encounter becomes a reminder of the Divine.

"You bathed?" he asked with a smile.

I nodded.

"Come, sit, have something to eat," he said.

Sitting in the sun on the porch were a handful of travelers waiting to be served. These included several Indians, a Japanese couple, an American couple with a young boy, and a Swiss man.

Soon, a teenage Tibetan boy brought us each a plate of rice, dahl, chapattis, and a glass of water. We all ate in silence, enjoying the panorama of mountains and forest under a clear, deep blue sky. The summer sun had risen, and a warm, gentle breeze rustled the trees on the ashram grounds, accenting the peace of that scene.

After a few minutes, we were joined by the Swami. He had changed into a nicer outfit, and I got a different impression of him. Swami Atmasvarupananda, with his jet-black shoulder-length hair and full, black beard, was a striking and charismatic man.

After some pleasantries, I asked him if he knew of any caves I might live in to do spiritual practices. He said he did not, and explained that Gangotri is only open from May through October. (The rest of the year it is buried in snow and inhabited by only a handful of hardy sadhus.*) He said the sadhus who had come to Gangotri in May (it was now June) had already occupied all of the available caves.

Nonetheless, reluctant to leave me hopeless in my quest, he suggested I ask at an ashram across the river, the Shivananda Yoga Vedanta Ashram, which did have a few

---

* A sadhu is one dedicated to a life of spiritual practice, having renounced possessions and life in society.

caves. He warned me, though, that these were normally reserved only for Indian sadhus. With this slim lead, I finished my breakfast and set out for the Shivananda Yoga Vedanta Ashram.

Not only did I want a cave; I needed one. I had come to Gangotri with precious little money. In fact, I had come to India with only enough to make a rather large donation to Amma's ashram so my wife, two daughters, and I could live there indefinitely. Our remaining savings were for our daughter's comfort, education, and any unforeseen expenses. That meant I was traveling on an extremely tight budget. This was okay with me since I had come to Gangotri as a spiritual seeker. Without credit cards and disposable cash, this forced me to rely on grace and not the power of the dollar. I realize this may sound extreme, but for me, it was a bit of an experiment too. What kind of support would I find? Would my intention for a retreat be blessed with a cave? If not, my sojourn would be a short one.

Krishnashram was the cheapest place to stay in Gangotri—the cost of room and board was by donation—but the Swami had confided to me the previous evening that an appropriate minimum donation would be 60 rupees a night (about $1.70 at the time). Although this included two meals, it was still more than twice what I had figured on spending, given my negligible budget. This only confirmed my need to find a cave, at any cost. That is, so long as it was free.

I crossed over the bridge that led to the Gangotri temple, an impressive old structure built of grayish white rock, and headed upstream. Just beyond the temple, I saw a Western man and woman in their mid-thirties sitting outside a tiny hut beside the Ganga. I stopped to talk with them and learned that they were from Switzerland and had already been in Gangotri for over a month. They also had hoped to stay in a cave, but had found none available. "We looked for three weeks, but the sadhus have them all," the woman told me. With my hopes dimming fast, I continued towards Shivananda Ashram.

As I approached the ashram gate, a middle-aged Indian Swami in faded ochre robes exited the gate heading in my direction. Thin from austerities, his soft eyes and gentle smile radiated a peaceful glow of much meditation.

"Om Namah Shivayah," I said, greeting him.

Beneath a thin, scraggly beard, his face shone with innocent joy. "Hari Om," he said in a quiet, shaky voice, as if he was breaking a long vow of silence.

I informed him of my intentions to meditate in a cave and also mentioned that I had been living in an ashram for two years (to let him know that I was not just a tourist looking for a cheap, dirty room). I gave it everything I had—exuded all the peace, serenity, and purity I possibly could.

He was friendly, but told me he didn't know of anything. Then, as an afterthought, he said, "You might ask Avadhuta Baba. Perhaps he will help you."

"Avadhuta Baba?" I asked.

"Just stay on this trail, and you'll come to his hut on the left. You can't miss him. He wears nothing."

"Om Namah Shivayah," I said. As hopeless as finding a cave had begun to seem, this mention of Avadhuta Baba was the first ray of light.

I continued along the trail, which followed the river upstream. The air was crystal clear, the sky deep blue, and the sun bright on the white and tan rocks and boulders all around me. Cave or no cave, I was glad I had come to Gangotri.

Through the brush and trees that grew along the trail, I spotted someone approaching me from the opposite direction.

A moment later, a pleasant, older Indian man in city clothes greeted me with the standard, "Hari Om."

"Hari Om," I returned. "Excuse me. I am looking for an empty cave. Do you happen to know of any?"

"No, I'm sorry," he said, "but you should ask Avadhuta Baba. He will help you. Just continue on this trail."

I began to wonder who this baba was, who everyone seemed to hold in such high regard as the solution to any problem. I could only hope he happened to have an extra cave.

Finally, I came to a clearing by the side of the Ganga, a beautiful and peaceful hermitage nestled amidst a grove of birch trees. There, in the sunlight, on a sheepskin, sat a naked Indian man in his early fifties. This, I took it, was Avadhuta Baba.

Removing my sandals, I sat a respectful four or five feet from the naked saint. He was not a particularly imposing figure—short, perhaps 5'4", dark-skinned, and balding. What hair he did have was long and matted, reaching below his shoulders. His beard was also long and graced with tufts of gray. Though not fat, his belly was what some Indians tactfully refer to as "well-nourished."

His eyes met mine. They twinkled with a knowing smile, and he graciously indicated a piece of carpet beside him for me to sit on.

As I moved to the piece of carpet, he picked up a knife and began to peel a cucumber with great care. I felt a tangible air of peace and spiritual energy about him. Slicing the cucumber into four sections, he offered me two of them, keeping two for himself. We ate in silence, watching the Ganga rush by, while a faint breeze gently blew through the birch trees. Now and then, he examined me and smiled. I felt completely at ease with him, as if we were old friends.

Soon an Indian disciple of his who spoke English joined us. Avadhuta Baba pointed to the man. Addressing me, he nodded and with a smile said, "Speak."

"Swamiji," I said, "I have come here from an ashram in Kerala, where I live with my teacher, to do a meditation retreat.

The baba asked a question in Hindi.

"What is your guru's name?" translated his disciple.

"Mata Amritanandamayi," I said.

"Mata Amritanandamayi," Avadhuta Baba repeated with a delighted smile. As he said Amma's name, I felt a wave of her presence, as if he was a mirror reflecting her consciousness to me.

"Do you know Amma?" I asked.

The translator said that Avadhuta Baba did not.

"What is Avadhuta Baba's* name?" I asked.

"Swami Dineshananda," replied the translator.

The baba again said something in Hindi.

"*Dina,*" began the translator, "means day; *Isha* means lord; *Dinesha* means 'lord of the day,' that is, the sun, who brings light. *Ananda,* as you know, means bliss. The Swami shines like the sun, radiating bliss."

The baba's name was well chosen, for I was certainly feeling the bliss of his presence. I would later learn that this humble man, sitting here with just one disciple and myself (I was used to the crowds of thousands around Amma), was actually one of the more revered figures in this area of the Himalayas. He was a guru to disciples from all over northern India.

I decided it was time to pop the question.

---

* Avadhuta Baba was a popular way to refer to Swami Dineshananda—as well as many other saints in India. It means a holy man who is above the ordinary codes of society.

"Does Swamiji know of an empty cave I might use for my retreat?"

"No, sorry," came the reply.

My heart sank.

Dinishananda looked at me with soft eyes and said a few words to the translator.

"Swami Dinesha says you may stay in a tent for a week as his guest. He is sorry he cannot accommodate you any longer than that, for the local people would think he was taking money from you. That would cause trouble for the Swami."

I considered this offer for a moment. I appreciated the baba's sweetness, but clearly he was stretching in making it. I did not want to be a burden. Besides, I wanted a cave for much longer than a week.

"Please thank Swami Dineshananda for his generous offer, but I will keep looking for a cave where I can stay for a long time."

Dineshananda again said a few words to the translator.

"Swamiji gives his blessings to your retreat. You may come whenever you like and meditate here. You may also ask him any questions. Please come often."

I thanked them.

Swami Dineshananda quickly rose to his feet and motioned for me to follow him. He led me down a short trail to a small hut, situated just above the Ganga. Even for a hut in rural India, this was rustic, roughly built with sticks, rocks, and an old, torn, cotton dhoti.* With a motion of his hand, he invited me to get in.

"Meditation room," he said in clear English with a charming smile and a twinkle in his eyes.

---

* A piece of material tied around a man's waist that covers his legs, similar to a long skirt.

"Om Namah Shivayah," I said, saluting him with joined palms. Then I crawled into the "hut," sat in lotus posture, and closed my eyes to meditate.

As I sat, I felt filled by the grace of Dineshananda. My meditation was deep and sublime. It occurred to me that this humble Swami had hidden his high spiritual state while talking to me, but now I was reaping the benefits of having sat in his presence for so long.

At one point, after about forty-five minutes, the bliss of meditation began to soften my heart. Suddenly, I became aware of my arrogance in insisting on having my own cave.

Who am I to expect my own cave? What makes me think I even deserve one? Sadhus (I had learned) spent months digging these caves out from under huge boulders; here I waltzed into town and expected to find one, pronto. How could God support such an attitude?

At this thought, I felt humbled. I would accept whatever God provided. If I had to, I would take my retreat in Krishnashram where I was already staying. It was touristy, certainly not secluded, but it would do in a pinch. At least I was in the Himalayas, and after all, it was nearly as rustic as a cave. I would not be able to stay as long as I had hoped because of the cost, but if that was what God provided, so be it.

I ended my meditation feeling that my whole attitude had been washed clean. There could be no doubt that the grace of the Swami had been instrumental in this meditation.

Crawling out of the hut into the brilliant afternoon sun, I stood for a few moments surrounded by the rugged mountain peaks jutting into the clear, blue sky. Birch trees rustled gently in the breeze. The Ganga danced and splashed before me, as I savored the solitude, holiness, and beauty of that place. Now, with my heart opened, it seemed all the more wondrous.

Pilgrims visiting such sacred spots consider their life fulfilled. Perhaps it is true; what I felt in that moment was indeed something rare. Such spots have offered their beauty and solitude to thousands of sincere seekers. They have been the resort of saints and sages throughout the ages, and are adorned with a vibration of sanctity. To stay even for a few days amidst that beauty, to bathe and drink of that holy river, to see the valleys of flowers and gaze on the peaks of the Himalayas was indeed a blessing. Filled with gratitude, I quietly left the Swami's hermitage and began the walk back to Krishnashram.

Always pray with full faith,
For the Infinite is within each particle of creation
And Her will can manifest at any moment.
Or don't pray for anything.
Just have full faith and the innocence of heart
To accept what comes.

The following morning, I decided to return to Swami Dineshananda and thank him for his blessing, which had been humbling and brought peace to my heart. As a token of appreciation, I brought him a few bananas.

As I approached his hermitage, I saw that he was surrounded by a handful of his devotees. They were all busily preparing lunch together. Unnoticed, I placed the bananas on a cloth spread on the ground for the other food, and then went to the little hut to meditate. After a couple of hours of blissful meditation, I returned to Krishnashram.

As I walked up to the ashram courtyard, I encountered the Swiss man who was also staying at Krishnashram. He was washing his clothes at a spigot just outside my room. His tall, lean, tanned frame was shirtless in the hot afternoon sun, and his long, brown hair reached well below his shoulders.

"Om Namah Shivayah," I said.

He raised his head. "Hari Om!" he returned with a friendly smile.

Whereas in the South, "Om Namah Shivayah," was more common, clearly here, "Hari Om," was the standard.

We introduced ourselves—his name was Philippe—and made friendly small talk for a while, which was inevitably easy with fellow seekers who came to the Himalaya, but especially so in this case. I had lived in Switzerland for a couple of years with Maharishi Mahesh Yogi in the 1970's, and Philippe and I enthusiastically compared notes on our favorite Swiss towns. At one point, I mentioned I was looking for an empty cave.

He started. "Eh?" he said, standing up straight and abandoning his laundry for a moment. "Someone told me just this morning they had seen an empty cave along a nature walk."

"Really?"

"Yes, the Japanese guy. You've seen him; he does asanas in that field every morning," he said, pointing to a field adjacent to the ashram.

"Did he say where the cave was?" I asked.

"He said it was all the way to the end of a trail."

"Which trail?"

"I don't know, but that's his room," he said pointing. "You should ask him."

"Thank you!" I said, and went to follow this new lead. I knocked at the door. It opened a moment later to reveal a Japanese woman.

"Is your husband here?" I asked.

"No," she said. "He's out hiking."

"Oh." To have to wait till his return was unthinkable. That could be hours. "Did he happen to mention anything about an empty cave?"

"No, I'm sorry."

"Which way does your husband walk in the morning?"

She pointed downstream, a direction I had yet to explore.

"Thank you!" I said with renewed hope, and headed downstream.

After crossing a bridge over a rushing stream, I came to the trailhead. I strode briskly through a beautiful forest of pines and Indian cedars, keeping my eyes peeled for any sign of a cave. I saw cascading waterfalls, gorgeous mountain views, idyllic meadows, rockslides, but no caves.

I had walked twenty minutes or so when I came to an area marked by a distinct silence and peace. The top of a boulder to my right, sunk deep into a hillside and surrounded by pines, caught my eye. I left the trail and walked down a short but steep hill along the edge of the sunken boulder. Reaching its base, I turned, and saw there, dug out from underneath the boulder . . . a cave!

It appeared deserted. Though its small door was fitted with a chain for locking, no lock was present, and the chain dangled uselessly. Crouching to fit through the half-sized door, I went in. Sure enough, it was uninhabited.

This was the first sadhu's cave I had ever been in. The walls and floor were bare dirt, and the ceiling was the bottom of the huge boulder overhead. It was nearly the size of a single-car garage, though I could not stand up straight without hitting my head on the bottom of the boulder. Water dripped from the ceiling, and the air was dank. The cave was basically a cold, dirty hole under a rock—perfect for a human-sized rodent. I imagined meditating and sleeping day and night in that cold hole smelling of musty earth. I shuddered. Surely that was not my fate in Gangotri. No, I would keep looking for a better cave.

Returning to the main trail, I continued in search of the supposed vacant cave spotted by the Japanese man. A half kilometer or so later, the trail ended at a spectacular canyon running perpendicular to the canyon carved by the Ganga. To my right, at the corner cliff-top where the two canyons met, flew an orange flag over a large boulder, marking the site of another cave. Since it was at the end of the trail, this must have been the cave the Japanese fellow had found. I would later learn that it was called Pandu Guha.*

I entered the cave, and to my dismay, there sat a Swami accompanied by two young, sharply dressed Indian men, who I took for college students.

"Hari Om!" the Swami called out to me, so loudly that I started. He was large and well-muscled, clad in a dirty orange shirt and dhoti. His hair was medium length and curly, his beard short. He was an imposing and handsome man.

---

* The word guha means cave. This one is named after the Pandavas of *Mahabharata* fame (the *Bhagavad-Gita* is a tiny part of the *Mahabharata*, the longest epic in the world). It is said that some 5,000 years ago, the heroes of the *Mahabharata*—Arjuna, his brothers, and their wife Draupadi—rested in this cave after retiring from the world on their final ascent to heaven (speculated by some to be in the area of nearby Tibet).

"Hari Om, Swamiji," I returned quietly. "Do you speak English?"

"Um, little," he said in a stentorian voice.

"You live here?" I asked.

"Yes!" he boomed.

"What do you want?" one of the students asked me. "I'll translate for you."

"I am looking for an empty cave."

"Why do you want a cave?" interjected the other student.

"To meditate in," I answered. Then, indicating the Swami with a gesture of my hand, I asked, "Is this your guru?"

"No!" responded the first student with disdain. "I don't believe in gurus."

He was so reactive to the idea of a guru, and seemingly so oblivious to any possible advantage, that I could not resist gently challenging him. "A true guru can help you in your growth."

"I have no use for gurus," he replied, his contempt unabated, "but I am interested in learning meditation. Could you teach me to meditate?"

"I could, but it would take some time, a few days at least." Whenever I taught meditation, I always ensured that my students came away not only knowing how to meditate, but understanding the mechanics of meditation thoroughly. In this way, they were prepared to meditate on their own for a lifetime. This takes a number of hours of instruction.

"Oh, we are going today," he said.

The Swami had been listening quietly, I assumed without understanding any of it. Now he abruptly got up, grabbed his bamboo walking stick, and walked out of the cave.

I turned to the student next to me. "Can you ask him if he knows of an empty cave?"

We all followed the Swami out of the cave, and the student spoke to him in Hindi. In response, the Swami turned to me and said, "I help you. Come."

The students wandered off, and the Swami quickly headed up along the edge of the canyon that ran perpendicular to the Ganga. I struggled to keep up.

At one point, he stopped. With a sweep of his hand, he introduced me to the cascading river several hundred feet below us. "*Rudra* Ganga," he said.

"Rudra Ganga," I repeated, nodding.

Then he pointed to the distant canyon wall on the opposite side of the river. "Cave," he said.

I carefully examined the cliffs he was pointing to, and there, just above the river, was a dark hole in the canyon wall.

"Englishman stay, uh, 6 months," he said.

I wasn't sure if he meant that an Englishman *had* stayed there for six months, would be coming *in* six months, or would be coming soon *for* six months. I decided that was all beside the point, as the cave seemed nearly inaccessible.

"How do you get to that cave?" I asked.

He pointed up the mountain next to us. "Go far up, then down. Very difficult."

"Ah." This might have been feasible were I cooking for myself, which I was not at all prepared to do, but I could never make that climb every day to go into town for food. "Any other caves?" I asked.

"Yes." He turned and began briskly walking through the forest towards town. Several times he stopped to show me some broken half-caves. Basically, these were piles of rocks next to overhanging cliffs or at the base of large boulders. Perhaps they had once served as caves, but now the rocks that had formed their walls were scattered in disarray. These would require extensive repairs, and in the meantime, I would be exposed to weather and wild animals. They were also an open invitation to theft.

Noting my lack of enthusiasm after showing me several such hovels, he said, "One more," and he continued leading me.

Despite his scanty English and my non-existent Hindi, we conversed as we walked. I liked him; he was extremely friendly and his face shone with a marked spiritual light. His name was Swami Krishnadas. He told me he had been a Swami for only a couple of years, having left his wife, two adult children, and all worldly possessions to lead the spiritual life of a wandering Sannyasin.*

When I heard this, I could not help but wonder about his family. He looked to be about my age, mid-forties. His children may have been grown, but they couldn't have been that old. Didn't they miss him terribly? Didn't he miss them? And how was his wife faring without him? I could only hope he had somehow provided for them.

"Are you in touch with your family? Don't they miss you?" I asked.

"Family doing fine," he said.

Though curious to know more, I decided it really wasn't my place to pry further.

Before long, we came to the very cave I had discovered on my own just an hour earlier. We crouched down and entered the cave together.

"First-class guha," he said, introducing me to the spacious cave with a graceful wave of his hand.

Suddenly, through his eyes, I realized he was right. This was quite a nice cave, as caves go. It was nearly as nice as

---

* One who has been initiated into Sannyasa, complete renunciation of the world; a Swami.

19

his own famous Pandu Guha. Now I hardly even noticed the cold and the dank smell.

"No one lives here?" I asked.

"Empty," he said simply.

"It's all right if I take it?"

"All right," he nodded affirmatively and walked out.

Outside the cave, we silently surveyed the towering cliffs rising perhaps 1,000 feet above us on the other side of the Ganga.

"You like cave?" he asked me.

"Yes, very nice. Perfect," I found myself saying.

He smiled. "Thank you," he said.

Before I could figure out why he had thanked me, he turned and began walking towards town. I followed him.

One concern I had about living in a cave was danger from wild animals. I had heard that tigers roamed these forests. In fact, that was my one unspoken fear—meeting a tiger in close quarters. The prospect struck me as more than a little intimidating. I decided that this was as good a chance as any to find out what I was in for.

"Are there any tigers around here?" I asked casually.

"No tigers."

He seemed certain about it.

"How about bears?"

"Uh . . ." he began thoughtfully. Then came his decided reply, "Bears no disturb sadhaks."*

I had to wonder, *how will the bears know I'm a sadhak?*

When we reached town, he turned to me and said, "I eat now. Thank you."

---

* A sadhak, in modern usage, is a dedicated spiritual aspirant who may or may not have renounced active life in the world. It is a more general term than sadhu, who has specifically renounced the world and therefore is also an ascetic.

I saluted him with joined palms, smiled with gratitude, and said, "Hari Om." He went to get his daily meal, and I went to my ashram room to meditate.

The next morning I told Philippe about my success in finding a cave. Philippe surprised me by graciously offering to help me move into my new abode.

"Are you sure?" I asked.

"I've never been in a cave," he said.

We strode through the forest together and when we arrived at the cave, we began cleaning out fallen rocks and a few branches that had somehow found their way inside. As Philippe and I spread pine needles over the cave floor to provide a semi-clean carpet over the dirt, I realized how fortunate I was.

I had probably found the one, vacant, intact cave in all of Gangotri—and it was free of charge. It had a door that locked no less. A more secluded, peaceful spot could not be imagined, for the only other person living in the entire forest was Swami Krishnadas. His presence over half a kilometer away was hardly a disturbance; rather, it was comforting. With the Ganga roaring in the canyon below, surrounded by gorgeous pine forests, towering cliffs, and snow-capped mountains, what more could I ask for? How perfect this was!

How I had found the cave also seemed a miracle: That I had left the trail at just that point to inspect the inconspicuous boulder after walking a mile from town. Then that I would meet Krishnadas, who would first show me broken remnants of caves and at last bring me back to see this one, so I could see it for what it was—a gift of grace. Not only was I shown the cave in its true light as a gift, but I could now see the real obstacle to receiving grace: My ego and prima donna attitude. Clearly this attitude had put me out of sync with the grace that ruled this sacred valley.

I thought of the Sanskrit word for divine grace, *anugraha*. It actually means "that which follows grasping."

Only when grasping ends and your heart opens, can you innocently receive the grace that surrounds you at all times.

I had never heard it explained that way, but it made sense to me.

Now everything was lining up to support my stay in Gangotri, even my food. Upon checking out of Krishnashram, I had made a small donation. Swami Atmasvarupananda had placed the hundred rupee notes in a cash box.

"Hari Om," he had said softly.

"Hari Om," I replied.

"So, you found a cave," he said with a smile.

"Yes. It's perfect."

"Very good," he said with a wobble of his head. "Are you sure you want to stay in a cave? Caves are very cold. Even the sadhus usually prefer huts and ashrams."

I had absolutely no doubt. "I like the solitude," I said. "And this way I can afford to stay here in Gangotri and do my sadhana* for longer. I only have to buy food now."

For a moment, he was thoughtful. Then he said, "At lunch every day the ashram makes an annakshetra (soup kitchen) for the sadhus here. You can come and eat with them. You don't have to pay. You can come for a meal every day for as long as you stay in Gangotri."

I could hardly believe it. Now I could afford to stay in Gangotri and pursue my spiritual practices for as long as I wanted. What a blessing!

"Hari Om!" I said in thanks.

---

*   Sadhana refers to dedicated spiritual practice.

22

Breathing in the sweet fragrance of the pine forest around my new abode, I once again felt humbled and grateful for all I had been given. A cave—and free meals. All this good fortune seemed a gift of divine grace.

Surrender your desire
Grace is courted not by pushing or grasping,
But by innocent gratitude.

CHAPTER 3

Loving Nature

While helping to clean and prepare the cave, Philippe mentioned that he had wondered what it was like to live in a cave. I invited him to spend the night. He wasn't sure he wanted to—while spreading pine needles, we had come across a few black scorpions—but in the end, he decided to join me.

Just before leaving Kerala, I had read a book written by a Swami who had wandered through the Himalayas one summer with only one wool blanket. Based on this, I had naively figured that a thin blanket (and a half-size Therm-a-Rest® as a mattress) would be sufficient for me as well. Not so. Though it was almost summer, nights at 10,000 feet in the Himalayas were wintry, and with only a thin blanket I froze. Even in his light down sleeping bag, Philippe was nearly too cold to sleep. Caves, we learned, are natural freezers.

Once we'd finished morning meditation, we walked to town and ate at Krishnashram's annakshetra. I bought another blanket and a few supplies I needed. After bidding adieu to Philippe, who had already had enough of cave living, I headed back through the forest to my new home.

Entering the dimly lit cave, I sat on the pine needles, savoring the solitude and silence. Slowly my eyes adjusted to the darkness. I inaugurated my retreat with a mental vow to maintain silence from that moment until I left Gangotri. I would not speak a word.

This might seem extreme, but I had experienced the benefits of maintaining silence many years before when I was undergoing training to teach meditation. Then I had taken silence for just one week, and it had quieted my mind and deepened my meditations to a remarkable extent. I had no idea what the effect of taking silence for many weeks would be, but I could hardly wait to find out.

With my meal still digesting, I was not yet ready to meditate. I wrapped myself in my Himalayan wool shawl, grabbed my newly purchased official Himalayan bamboo walking stick, and left the cave to explore the area.

The warm June afternoon was fragrant with pine, cedar, and thyme, which grew wild and covered the ground in that area of the forest. The sound of the rushing Ganga was at first barely noticeable, but grew louder as I walked. Finally, I came to a spot where the trees opened to reveal a stunning canyon. Brown and white cliffs rose above me, the sun playing on their sheer faces. Here and there, wind-twisted pines adorned those cliff faces, boggling the mind: How could they gain a foothold on barren rock? Below me, the sacred river thundered through the canyon, exploding with power.

I watched as mammoth boulders challenged the furious Ganga in its course, but the river prevailed, leaping over them in lofty waves and splashes as it had throughout the ages. The surrounding mountains and pines stood in mute witness to Ganga's conquest. The whole scene brimmed with the power and drama of nature.

I sat on a smooth, white boulder and for perhaps forty minutes drank in that scene through all my senses, as the wind from the canyon buffeted me. Finally, I closed my eyes to meditate.

In moments, my body and mind filled with a spiritual energy so powerful my body could barely contain it. It radiated all around me, holding me in what seemed to be a tangible field of grace. But it was so strong, I also felt as if I might burst into pieces or as if that energy might physically lift me from the ground. In fact, it seemed surprising that my body was not actually shooting into the sky, so intense was the energy. My friend who had recommended I come here was right. It was an amazing place for spiritual practice; clearly, the power of that valley was magnifying my inner experience.

Energy is real, and meditation makes you more sensitive to it. For thousands of years, India's yogis have explored the reality of subtle energy, or prana (life-breath), which moves through subtle channels in the body (nadis). The prana, nadis, and chakras are all part of the energetic system within the human body, the so-called pranic or energetic body.

When the energy is awakened during meditation, you may feel heat, tingles, or a sense of fullness and solidity in the body. It will cause you to sit up with perfect posture without any exertion; it simply feels more natural to sit up straight. You may feel lightness, as if you're about to rise into the air like a dandelion spore floating on the breeze, or you may feel solid as a boulder. You will feel your senses and mind enlivened and clarified by the energy, and as you become even more familiar with subtle energy, you will realize that energy, clearly experienced, is intense bliss. You will feel that bliss tangibly throughout your being.

When that energy is fully enlivened and flowing in an unrestricted and balanced way, it is said to create optimal health, higher consciousness, and access to hidden creative potentialities, including supernormal abilities. But most importantly, the buildup of energy gradually opens the higher centers of consciousness that allow you to live in the presence of the Divine, and eventually to realize your own higher Self, the Essence of all existence.

There are techniques you can do to specifically enliven the subtle energy in the body and direct it to clear and open the chakras. India's most accomplished yogis are great observers of the subtler aspects of human existence, specifically the relationship between mind, body, breath, and energy. Over the centuries, they've developed a myriad of techniques that work with these relationships to develop higher consciousness. I practiced and taught many of these techniques. It is a fascinating science.*

Soon the energy settled. My mind melted into a blissful unboundedness, and my body felt as solid as the boulders scattered around me. The wind from the canyon blasted me with cold, but I remained untouched, unmoved, absorbed in that inner firmament, the space of pure consciousness.

The clouds parted, and the sun caressed the earth with warmth. I opened my eyes. The sun was directly before me, shining just above the mountain peaks, a brilliant jewel displayed against the velvet of surrounding dark clouds. The steady roar of the river from below now seemed musical,

---

* See www.ajayan.com for a free guided meditation that gives a taste of this science. If you wish, you can also access detailed video instruction (in my membership site) in the best forms of meditation I've found, and the most effective techniques for working with the energetic body. These techniques are a great blessing of the Yoga and Tantric traditions of India and help make meditation deep and effortless.

like a symphony's inspired crescendo, sounding on and on. I had entered another world, a heaven, in which my senses were all cleared and enlivened. And in that moment, I was struck by a simple truth:

> *To spend time in the beauty and power of nature is to allow nature to awaken its beauty and power within us.*

This was not arrived at rationally; rather, sitting on the edge of that canyon, it was a self-evident truth. It was my experience. Without any intention on my part, that place was filling me with its power and beauty. Somehow, opened by the meditation, I was one with that power and beauty.

> *The Infinite has created nature. The intricate beauty of nature is available to all of us. Why not take advantage of this gift, breathe it in, absorb it? Not that we all must go to the Himalayas. We can find the gift of nature in our backyard or in a city park. To spend even twenty minutes each day in a garden, lavishly appreciate its wonders, its fine details, even one blossom, one leaf, a bird's flight through the air—this will open our eyes to the Divine.*

At sunset, I returned to my cave. Wrapping myself in a blanket over my wool shawl and putting on my wool hat and gloves, I sat and meditated into the night.

Over the next week, my daily routine became established. I typically woke at around 3:30 a.m. and started my morning meditation. At sunrise, I took a break to do some *yogasanas* (yoga postures) and *pranayama* (yogic breathing); then continued meditating until 9:30. For my daily meal, I walked through the forest to Krishnashram's annakshetra (soup kitchen), where Basmati rice and dahl were served at 10 a.m. A few times a week, I added to this some curried potato and peas bought at a tea stall in town.

After my meal, I walked each day to the Ganga for my daily bath, washed clothes, and filtered a supply of Ganga water for drinking. Returning to the cave, I wrote in my journal and took a nature walk until 3 or 4 p.m.; then I did more yoga and pranayama and meditated until about 9 p.m. Finally, I read the *Ribhu Gita** by candlelight and meditated some more until going to sleep. Thus, I managed to meditate about 12 hours a day.

This routine lasted as long as I was in Gangotri, with one exception. After a couple of weeks, I found myself becoming weaker, until one morning I found it difficult to walk to town for my meal. A single meal was simply not enough for me in the cold climate. From then on, I took a light bedtime snack of fruit, or some honey and ghee spread on a chapatti. Eventually, I discovered patches of wild sorrel along the mountain path on the way to town, and I sometimes topped a chapatti with this leafy green vegetable to make a sandwich.

---

* A classic Indian text that expounds a pure expression of Advaita, or non-dualism, the philosophy that all existence is nothing but Brahman, one's own innermost Self.

This simple routine and diet, in silence and solitude, left my mind directed solely to my purpose of diving deep and realizing the Self. Well, almost . . .

Living in a cave was not all natural beauty and savoring the Divine in solitude. It was damned cold! Though it was June and temperatures might reach 75 degrees Fahrenheit in the sun in the afternoon, in the cave it would never get above 50. At night, temperatures in my little hovel were nearly freezing, and the damp air inside made it seem even colder. Wearing everything I had brought with me—including several shirts, a sweater, a sweatshirt, two pairs of pants, a wool ski hat and gloves—and then covering myself in three blankets and a shawl, all topped with a rain poncho, I managed to stay just warm enough to sleep through the night. It took me half an hour each night to get dressed for bed.

Meditating in my cave

Caves are also home to bugs, beetles, mice, and scorpions. The beetles particularly liked to join me in bed; fortunately, the scorpions kept to themselves. Another problem was dirt. Caves are dirty, and somehow it found its way into everything—my bed, pack, clothes, socks, and shoes. Every day I had to wash my white clothes in the Ganga. The icy river froze my fingers blue in seconds.

Washing my clothes in the Ganga

That first week in my cave, many times I wondered how long I would last. *Why should I put myself through this? Is it really worth it? If only I could borrow a propane heater from some ashram or hotel.* It seemed an entirely reasonable request under the circumstances: "Excuse me. I'm living in a cave and it's very cold. Could you lend me a propane heater?"

I woke up and opened my eyes. It was still dark. For a while I lay there, contemplating whether to go back to sleep or sit up and meditate. I was passably warm; to sit up would no doubt change that. I turned on the flashlight I kept by my pillow and exhaled across the width of the cave. Sure enough, the cloud of steam from my breath nearly reached the far wall. This was how I measured the temperature each morning.

Eventually, I sat up on my Therm-a-Rest®, got into lotus position (your basic pretzel meditation pose), folded one blanket to cover my legs and wrapped myself in a shawl and the other two blankets, and began to do some pranayama (yogic breathing) and other techniques* to awaken the subtle energies and direct them upwards to clear and open the chakras (centers of energy and higher consciousness).

Over the years, I had learned many such practices, but stuck with the half-dozen I really liked. Depending on the technique, it could be energizing, or soothing and calming. Always, they put me into a state of deep inner stillness, silence, and expansion; my mind calm and peaceful, but also boundless, like space.

After 15 minutes or so of these practices, I began to meditate. Instantly, I found myself floating in an inner

---

*   Combinations of bandhas (locks) that awaken and direct subtle energies, and mudras, gestures to reflect subtle energies in specific ways. These become especially effective when combined with pranayama and meditation.

universe of silence that had little or nothing to do with the external world, my cave, or the cold.

It might seem that meditating 12 or more hours a day requires immense self-discipline. Enduring the cold *did* require discipline, but meditating hours every day does not. Does it require immense self-discipline to eat a heaping bowl of your favorite ice cream every day? That is what meditation becomes. You savor it. It's a hedonist's delight.

In case you have never meditated before, to give you some idea of what it's like, I like to use a metaphor. Think of the mind as an ocean. In fact, this is fairly accurate— the mind *is* an ocean, of consciousness. Most of the time we hang out on the surface of that ocean, moving from thought wave to thought wave. We also have very little control over our thoughts; we are washed this way and that by the rising and falling swells. This is what we experience more or less every waking hour of our lives. Meditation changes that. The moment we enter into true meditation, for perhaps the first time in our lives, we dip beneath the surface of that ocean.

When this first happens, it can be a wonderful surprise. As you dip beneath the surface of the thinking mind, you immediately feel a noticeable inner stillness and silence. Suddenly you are not being pushed around by the waves. You are in a space of peace. This doesn't mean that all the thought waves cease; thoughts can and will continue—the entire ocean does not suddenly become still—but you now have a different relationship with your thoughts. You are no longer caught by them. They float by overhead, on the periphery of the mind, while you descend into inner depths. As a result, you feel a deep silence, a mental and physical restfulness and relaxation that is wonderfully rejuvenating.

When I first started meditating in 1970, this experience of inner silence was not only relaxing, but pleasant. That pleasantness and the sense of healing, soothing silence encouraged me to stick with my daily practice. Gradually, over the years, the inner silence deepened and meditation became more than simply pleasant; it became blissful. Intensely, sweetly blissful, both mentally and physically. Sometimes that sweetness also contained a delectable fragrance of something so sublime it can only be described as divine.

More years of practice brought more clarity and depth, such that during meditation my body and mind were often drenched in soothing, sweet, and yet powerful, dynamic silence. I say "dynamic silence," because it is not just silence. It is silence permeated with intense, pure, blissful energy.

An ensemble of birds were now singing in the forest outside my cave. I opened my eyes a slit; sure enough, the first rays illumined the pine needles outside my cave door. The promise of warmth beckoned. I decided to move outside to do yoga in the sun.

I unrolled my yoga mat on top of a large moss-covered rock. For a few minutes, I basked in the warm, morning sunlight, breathing the fresh mountain air, rich with the fragrance of pine and a sweet smell like berries that I could not identify. Meditation had awakened all my senses. The fragrances of nature were intoxicating.

As I began the yoga postures, the giant boulder that formed the roof of my cave caught my attention. Its white and golden rock face gleamed in the sun. A deep green carpet of moss hid much of its face, and upon the moss, a net of fine spider webs catching the sun's rays appeared as strands of golden light. The rock and moss, the intricate spider's craft, every crevice in the boulder and each of its glimmering facets of quartz crystal, the shadow cast by overhanging pine branches—it was all a glorious work of art. The golden light of Divinity shone on the face of that boulder.

As I lay on my back for a shoulder stand, I noticed the pines rising above. They, too, shone with a wondrous light. The deep blue mountain sky, the gleaming sun, the billowing white clouds—they all shone with an ineffable, lustrous presence. Everything was bathed in love.

A phrase from the Bible came to mind: "You may hear and hear, but you will never understand; you may look and look, but you will never see. For this people's mind has become gross, their ears are dulled, and their eyes are closed. Otherwise, their eyes might see, their ears hear, and their mind understand . . ."*

What is it that we can hear but not understand, look at but not see, because the mind has become gross? Something subtle. Not just something subtle, but the subtlest, even beyond the subtlest. Surely Christ was speaking of the highest Truth, of life's hidden spiritual dimension. Was he not saying that we need only remove the grossness from our mind, make our mind fresh, innocent, and subtle through spiritual practices—prayer, devotion, fasting, meditation—and we will discover that truth in our own experience? We will hear the Divine, see the Divine, know that everything exists in divine love . . .

In that moment, I knew it could not be otherwise. The Himalayas were teaching me now, in their silence, their beauty. I had emerged from my cave to do yoga in the sun and to warm up, only to find that I was as deep in meditation as ever, with eyes open.

---

*   Matthew, 13:14-15

After asanas I went to town for my meal and bath, and then decided to walk to the canyon overlook where I had been so filled with the power of nature a few days before. On the way, I spotted a newly formed waterfall on the canyon wall opposite me, created by a landslide further up the mountain. The narrow stream plummeted over the canyon's edge, falling hundreds of feet in pearl-like drops to join the Ganga below. Blown by gusts of wind, the waterfall's spray formed a rainbow across the canyon.

It seemed to me that a more magical scene could hardly exist on this earth. I longed to simply sit and be part of it. A ledge jutted from the canyon wall ten feet below me, and a trail led down to it. Descending to the ledge, I sat on a bed of wild thyme covered with tiny purple blossoms.

Drinking the beauty of that scene, I felt as if I were more nature than man, more one with the wind, water, earth, light, than with my own body. Elation filled me. At one moment the thought came, "I love . . ." but then there was no particular thing I loved; rather, I loved everything. I loved life, being alive . . .

"Hari Om!" The call boomed like a crack of thunder from just behind and above me. It startled me so badly I nearly slipped off the canyon ledge.

Turning around, I saw a large dark-skinned figure in orange robes standing over me. Krishnadas.

"Sheeze!" I gasped under my breath, standing up to greet him as he climbed down to join me.

"Okay?" he asked me heartily.

I nodded enthusiastically, miming to him that I was in silence by pretending to zip my mouth shut with my fingers.

"Thank you," he said.

We stood side by side on the ledge and watched the waterfall without a word. My silence didn't matter; what could words add to that magnificent scene.

After a few minutes, Krishnadas climbed to the top of the canyon and disappeared from my view as he walked into the forest. I was grateful for his presence and his apparent concern for my welfare. His caring assured me that I had a spiritual brother in Gangotri.

Now it was time to meditate. I went to a spot just below my cave on the canyon's edge, spread my meditation blanket, and began. After about forty-five minutes, though, my eyes opened. The thought had suddenly struck me that I was sitting at the top of a trail to the river. If true, this would solve the biggest problem I had experienced with my cave: its lack of access to water for bathing, drinking, and washing clothes.

Though the Ganga flowed just a few hundred feet from my cave, nearly all of that few hundred feet was a sheer drop to the canyon floor. Thus, I had to get my water in town, a 20-minute walk each way, which in the coming rainy season would be a hassle. Having spent several afternoons trying to find a way to the river closer to the cave, I had finally given up. Every promising route ended in impossible danger. That stretch of the canyon had been perfectly designed to tempt, then frustrate, any and all attempts to gain access to the river.

I studied the narrow stretch of grass descending towards the canyon floor from where I sat. The grass was trampled a bit, probably by wild goats, but it indeed looked like a possible trail to the river—and here it was, just below my cave! How could I have missed it?

In my excitement, I quickly came out of meditation and made my way down the supposed trail. For a hundred feet, it was precarious but passable. Then it ended abruptly at the top of a slick, nearly vertical, ten-foot slide formed of smooth rock. Below the slide was a grass-covered ledge, and thirty feet below that was a gorgeous stretch of white sand along the shore of the Ganga. This was the closest I had gotten to the river without having to walk almost all the way to Gangotri. I could not believe that it was just one more dead end. It seemed to me that just out of my view, the trail must certainly continue from the grass ledge to that sandy beach.

With my eyes fixed on the seductive, white sand, I sat and began to lower myself carefully down the rock slide, my back to the rock, holding onto some grass clumps at the top of the ledge behind me. With my feet, I searched for a foothold. There weren't any. Suddenly, I realized that the drop to the grass-covered ledge was too high and too dangerous—but I had already passed the point of no return; my arms did not have the strength in that awkward position to lift me back to safety.

Panic hit me. My body tensed and my breath came in gasps. If I let go and slid down that rock face, I might never be able to get up again. The next moment, my arms and the grass clumps gave away together. I slid down the rock and landed on the grass ledge.

Shaken but uninjured, I saw in a moment that I had indeed reached a dead end. There was no more trail at all, just a 30-foot, sheer drop to the ground. Jumping down that was out of the question. I examined the slick rock face I had just slid down: no handholds. It was an impossible ascent. But I could not stay where I was; soon, the freezing cold of night would set in.

There had to be a way. I was not about to freeze to death on that ledge. Yet the chance of someone finding me before nightfall was nil. No one but Krishnadas and Philippe knew the whereabouts of my cave, and neither of them would ever come down that goat trail. I was also hidden from view of the opposite side of the canyon, where someone might otherwise have spotted me.

I considered calling for help, but the thundering of the river made that a hopeless prospect. Indeed, now the Ganga's deafening roar assumed an ominous pitch, drowning out all other sound, drowning out even my thoughts. It was likely that my body would not be found for weeks on that ledge. *What a fool! I never should have interrupted my meditation!*

Suddenly, the thin atmosphere at that altitude did not hold enough oxygen to feed my lungs. Of its own accord, my breathing became wild. I was panicking and hyperventilating. Turning to face the rock slide, I mentally said a moment's prayer and threw myself at it in a mindless scramble towards the top.

Amazingly—I have no idea how—I somehow reached high enough to grab a small grass clump near the top. The grass began to tear under my weight. Catching another clump with my other hand, I pulled with all my strength. Just as that grass clump gave way, I caught the roots of a small bush. I cursed myself under my breath. I could not believe that my carelessness had put me where my life relied upon a flimsy web of roots.

The roots and grass began to tear. I reached and grabbed another handful of grass. Planting my feet against the rock and pulling myself up, I rolled onto the top of the ledge.

As I lay there, my lungs heaving, my clothes covered with grass stains and dirt, I gave thanks from the depths of my being. Only by grace had I escaped disaster. Climbing that sheer rock wall without handholds looked practically impossible. Thoroughly shaken, I returned to my seat on the edge of the canyon to finish my meditation.

Now the beauty of the canyon and forest around me assumed a different light. The Himalayas were not just a beneficent gift of nature for all to appreciate. If you were careless, you could die here. No thoughtfully placed warning signs or rails checked the foolhardy. Magnificent beauty and power, yes, but the danger of those mountains was not to be disregarded.

An hour or so later, calmed and at peace, I opened my eyes. The sun was just setting. Around me was spread an exquisite garden of rock, moss, emerald grasses, and lofty pines, their limbs and needles aflame with sunlight. Once again, the sacred Ganga rushed happily through the canyon floor. Danger seemed far indeed from this place of beauty. Peace pervaded everything.

What human hand could form such a display of intricate splendor? Who, seeing this, could doubt the existence of a higher power? Then came a wave of love, a child's innocent love. But for grace, I would not even exist.

We are but children of Love.
What joy to be children, what solace,
What greater peace than to know
You are a child of the Infinite.

CHAPTER 4

Fathoming the Unfathomable

Reacting to anything whatsoever in our lives
Is the mind resisting the Real.
See your reaction, the self-imposed limits of ego,
Now feel who is seeing:
Your Self, unbounded, whole,
The same Self of whatever sparked your reaction.
You and That are one.

Nearly every day since moving into the cave, I had spent a little time with Philippe in town. Sometimes we would eat together, or just wash our clothes in the Ganga together. He was an aspiring *hatha yogi*, one whose path is primarily yoga postures. He was also one of the friendliest people I had ever met. Having hiked into Gangotri in late April, even before the road had opened, he seemed to know everyone. There was not a shopkeeper, sadhu, or beggar that did not light up with a smile the moment they saw him coming, and he got special prices from every restaurant in town.

My silence was no hindrance to our friendship, for Philippe was an expert mime interpreter. This is rare. I found that many people had difficulty understanding even my most obvious signals, while others simply refused to even try. Philippe's sincere effort to comprehend my mime acts seemed an expression of his innate friendliness, and his natural intelligence allowed him to immediately understand my intended meaning.

Eventually he, too, went into silence. Our "conversations" then became two-way mime shows on the stage of the shore of the Ganga while we washed our clothes. This created an amusing spectacle for onlooking sadhus. Sometimes our mime acts were complemented with hastily written notes on scraps of paper. Though no words were spoken between us, day-by-day our friendship deepened.

As far as we were concerned, our limited communication was not a compromise of our vows of silence. People take silence for various reasons, but we both did it to conserve the subtle energy that is utilized during everyday speech. This conserved energy deepens meditation as well as the inner silence of the mind. In spiritual traditions around the world, both East and West, a vow of silence usually allows for limited communication via notes or gestures.

One afternoon, through mime and notes, I encouraged Philippe to move into a half-cave near mine. He declined, scribbling on a paper that he was concerned about his belongings being exposed to theft. He added that he admired my trust in leaving my belongings in a cave, and pointed out that whereas the usual sadhu cave dweller had nothing to steal, a Westerner in a cave was an easy target. That thought, obvious as it was, had never occurred to me.

After bathing and washing my clothes, I returned to my cave alone. My pants had gotten muddy at the river, and while standing outside in the warm sun, I took them off to change. Just then, as I stood in the sun in my underwear, a loud voice from behind me called out, "Hari Om!"

Startled, I literally jumped. Immediately, I realized that Krishnadas had gotten me again. *Does he do that on purpose?* Next time, I told myself, I would not be taken by surprise.

Sure enough, the imposing figure of Krishnadas in orange robes appeared from behind a boulder. Another smaller Swami accompanied him.

"Hello," said Krishnadas warmly. "All right?"

I nodded, feeling more than a little uncomfortable standing there in my underwear. Nevertheless, out of regard for local customs of hospitality, with a wave of my hand I invited them into my cave.

Once inside, I began looking through my pack to find my last pair of pants. The two men watched, sitting silently on the pine-needle floor. I emptied my entire pack, but no pants. Where were they? My discomfort was increasing by the second.

"Sit," said Krishnadas in a kind tone.

I sat on my bed. Then I put my hand to my mouth as if I was eating, to ask if they wanted anything. Fortunately, I had bought two bananas in town that day for my bedtime snack.

They both declined by shaking their heads.

A few days before, I had seen the smaller Swami gathering firewood in the forest with Krishnadas. I took it that they were sadhana buddies and fellow disciples of the same guru. He was also friendly and very sweet. We sat in uneasy silence.

"Uh," began Krishnadas in a deep voice, struggling to communicate in English, "I going. Moving to Gangotri." He waved his hand in the direction of town.

I wanted to ask why, but being in silence, I could only nod that I understood. Actually, I think I knew why he was moving. His famous Pandu Guha was a tourist attraction, and sightseers must have been interrupting his spiritual practices. At least that's why I would have moved if I were him. (I later found out it was not the tourists, but increasing cold and rain with the approaching monsoon season that spurred him to move closer to town.)

News of his going saddened me. His presence had been comforting, as he had been the only other human living in the forest. He also seemed sad to be leaving this beautiful area of the woods. Placing my hand over my heart, I tried to convey with a smile my gratitude for his presence and concern. They both nodded and smiled warmly back. Then without a word, they rose, placed their hands over their hearts, turned and left.

Now I was completely isolated in that forest, which suddenly seemed lonely and desolate. The weather was also turning for the worse with the onset of the rainy season.

I finally found my pants (I had used them as a pillow for sleeping the night before), and began my routine of afternoon asanas. Then I decided to meditate in the cave, as it looked like it might rain. I wrapped up in my wool shawl, hat, and gloves, and began.

An hour or so passed of especially powerful and deep meditation, during which my mind seemed a gleaming jewel of divinity, shining in all directions. I had often felt filled with light in meditation, but this crystalline, divine radiance was particularly sublime.

I heard the unexpected crunch of footsteps just outside the cave. The next instant, a large, bearded man I had never seen before, dressed in a tattered orange dhoti and shawl, appeared at my open door. Both his clothes and face were stained dark with layers of dirt; he was in dire need of a good wash. "Hari Om!" he said in a deep voice.

Mentally, I moaned. Couldn't he see I was meditating? Maintaining my silence, I returned his greeting with folded hands and a nod.

The man stooped down at my door and, ignoring that I was obviously in the middle of meditation, began a lengthy conversation in Hindi. By the way he paused from time to time, I gathered he was asking questions. When I did not answer, he continued.

Finally, during one of his pauses, I went into my Marcel Marceau mime act. First I pretended to zip my mouth shut to let him know that I was observing silence. Then I shrugged my shoulders and raised my palms upward in a gesture that I hoped would communicate I didn't speak Hindi and couldn't understand a word he was saying.

He repeated his questions. I removed my hat to make sure he saw that I was a Westerner. I pointed to my head to emphasize the fact, and again shrugged my shoulders and raised both of my palms to convey my incomprehension, then pointed to my ears and shook my head in the negative. I figured that would let him know that I didn't know Hindi.

He continued talking rapidly in Hindi.

I nodded and closed my eyes as if to meditate, at which point he became quiet. Through a slit in my eyes, I saw him sit down on my doorstep.

After a few moments, he broke the silence. "Prasad?"*
he asked.

Ah, he wanted food.

I opened my eyes. All I had was ghee, honey, and the two bananas scheduled for my dinner. Offering him a spoonful of honey and ghee was certainly inappropriate, and though I wouldn't have minded sacrificing my

---

* A consecrated offering of food.

banana dinner for Krishnadas and his buddy, I was not so inclined for this uncomprehending lug. There was also something disquieting about him. Not only was he unkempt and dirty, but his red eyes betrayed his heavy use of marijuana. I also had the distinct feeling that if I gave him an inch, he would take over. Philippe's warning of Westerners in caves being targets for theft was not far in the back of my mind, especially now that I was alone in the forest.

I shook my head and mimed that I ate my meals in town (putting my hand to my mouth as if eating and then waving in the direction of Gangotri). This, after all, was true.

He pointed to the bag with my few foodstuffs in it.

Again, I shook my head and closed my eyes, hoping he would go away. Instead, he entered and made himself comfortable sitting a couple of feet in front of me. I continued to meditate while he sat waiting quietly.

Ten more minutes passed. I hoped he would get bored, but no such luck. Etiquette among sadhus probably required me to invite him to stay the night, but I dreaded the thought of sleeping with him in my cave. How would I get rid of him, and what did he want? I opened my eyes.

Immediately he pointed to my bed. "Sleeping?" he asked.

I nodded.

"Niiiice," he said in an ominous tone I had thought was reserved for bad guys in Italian Westerns. "Tomorrow I go Rishikesh," he continued, "need 150 rupees. You give. I go. No problem."

Ah, so that was it; he was after money. And did his statement hold something of an ultimatum?

Now my mind raced with speculation: Would he rob me if I didn't voluntarily give him the money? Or if I gave it to him, and he saw where I kept my wallet, would he try to steal the rest of my money? Even if he didn't rob me, only one hotel manager in all of Gangotri had been willing to cash my traveler's checks (and that at great inconvenience he did not wish to repeat), and I only had 300 rupees left. This I needed to supplement my meager diet. Was this sadhu's need greater than mine? After all, he didn't *have* to go to Rishikesh. He could stay in Gangotri, and as an Indian Sadhu, get multiple daily free meals at the various annakshetras (soup kitchens) in town.

I decided against taking the risk of giving him money. Shrugging my shoulders, I rubbed my thumbs and fingers together to indicate cash, then shook my head to show that I had none to spare.

"Tomorrow I go Rishikesh. You give 150 rupees," he insisted.

I shook my head again and pointed to the cave, then to myself, then to the cave again, hoping he would get the message that I, too, was on a tight budget.

He was silent for a moment. I took the opportunity to close my eyes and meditate. That is, pretend to meditate. Actually, I was weighing the odds that he would try to rob me. He was obviously an aggressive beggar, but was he a thief? The question had every cell in my body at the peak of alertness in an odd combination of fear and calculating calm. We were a good mile from town. No one would be walking in the woods at that time with darkness setting in and with the light rain that was now falling. He weighed probably twice as much as me. Still, I doubted that he would attack while I was meditating; hardly a thug in the entire country would be so sacrilegious as to do that. I decided my best bet was to keep my eyes closed and project all the inviolable serenity I could muster.

Another ten minutes passed in silence. He wasn't budging. Now my fear gave way to irritation, for I wanted to get on with my meditation in earnest. Besides, soon it would be pitch dark, and he would *have* to spend the night, for I could not push him out into the forest after nightfall. Deciding that it was time for action, I opened my eyes.

"You give 150 rupees," he said promptly, "no problem."

I shook my head and pulled my empty pants pocket inside out to show I was flat broke.

"150 rupees, no problem," he persisted.

That did it. Completely forgetting my fear, I hopped to my feet, firmly grabbed his elbow with my left hand, and with my right, grabbed my Himalayan bamboo walking stick. I gave him two taps with it on his back as I pulled him out the door.

Thankfully, he didn't resist. I closed the door and sat down to finish my meditation.

Was that it? Was it over?

"Hari Om," I heard him say through the door, "I going." "Hari Om," he repeated a few more times, "I going."

Clearly, he wasn't actually going until I said good-bye.

I opened the door and again greeted him with folded hands and a warm smile to show him there were no hard feelings. Then I waved good-bye, closed the door, and returned to my meditation—or rather, to sitting with my eyes closed listening intently for sounds of his presence outside.

I heard nothing. He was gone.

Now my whole being settled with relief, as if I had narrowly escaped disaster. Or had I? Had the danger been real or imagined? Should I have fed him? Should I have given him the 150 rupees, half of my remaining money? That would have been charitable, but it hadn't seemed right; to have even revealed my wallet to the fellow would have increased my vulnerability considerably.

My mind now uncontrollably pondered whether my treatment of the beggar (I use the term loosely; he seemed more a hustler than a beggar) had been appropriate. It is said in the *Mahabharata* that the highest purpose of wealth is to give in charity. The same text declares that misplaced charity injures both the giver and the recipient. The *Bible* says, "Be wise as serpents, yet harmless as doves." That is, there must be savvy in our meekness. Yet Christ also said, "Give when you are asked to give; and do not turn your back on a man who wants to borrow."*

The answer remained a mystery to me. Perhaps I should have given to him, shown him all hospitality. One banana wouldn't have hurt at all. Maybe, if I hadn't been so suspicious, he would have turned out to be a worthy friend. Maybe. But for a sadhu, his intentions and methods had been entirely inappropriate, if not sleazy. Still, hadn't my attitude towards this Swami been based in fear, which blocked my own unconditional love? Or was it appropriate wisdom? It seemed an unanswerable question, at least for me in that moment.

Then a verse from the *Bhagavad Gita* came to mind: "Action, indeed, must be known, as also wrong action and inaction. Incomprehensible is the way of action."† This is exactly what I felt. I needed to understand whether I had made a mistake in my actions with that Swami. Somehow my peace depended upon doing so. But no matter how hard I tried, I couldn't be sure of the answer. Indeed, the way of action was incomprehensible. So why had Krishna said that action must be known if it is incomprehensible?

For a few moments, my mind was suspended by this impenetrable koan. Then a faint light dawned:

---

*   Matthew, 5:42

†   *Bhagavad Gita,* IV:17

The answer to the unanswerable lies not in mere intellectual understanding, which is by nature incomplete. The answer lies in diving into life's contradictions, doing our best to understand, and when we can go no further, surrendering. This might not bring knowledge, but it humbles and opens us to life's mystery. Opened, we may see and hear more truly, and meet others with more humility and love. Only then can the miraculous happen: While yet remaining in mystery, we may live the benefit of knowing—that is, graceful, loving, and appropriate action.

The entire day's events had set me up. Philippe's warning, Krishnadas leaving me alone in the forest, the sleazy tactics of the begging Swami—all were perfectly designed to arouse my fear and distrust, to close me down. Why? That I might see where I was closed, so that something new would be forced to open inside me—the unknown.

I felt humbled. Certainly, there had to be a different way to respond. Fear and distrust were not the high road; they should not dictate my actions. If ever such a situation happened again, I would stay open to finding another way. I would set aside fear and take a more loving course, one that could bring out something higher in myself and the other person. Looking back on the beggar's visit, I saw that at least I could have shared my food. That would have been more gracious.

I found myself praying that I would be given another such encounter, another chance.

Know your Realization is incomplete
Until you behold this universe
Bathed in Love.

The next morning, after sunrise, I interrupted my meditation to move from the cave's frigid darkness into the warm sun outside.

I settled into my favorite spot on the canyon's edge and shed several layers of clothing needed in my cave. A fresh, cool breeze carried the fragrance of pine and cedar, while the Ganga roared below. Bugs flitted in the sunlight between the trees. Sitting in that mountain garden, I felt a wave of love for the beauty of nature around me.

What is holiness, but love for everything? Not simply to love, but to BE love that embraces all—every creature and every particle of creation—to be one with the love that has created all this.

As I continued sitting, an ant crawled on my arm. Carefully picking him up, I placed him in the grass.

Love cannot injure anything. How foreign even the killing of an ant would be to the Love that embraces all. So yes, *ahimsa* (non-injury to others in thought, word, and deed), is a starting point to become love. A vow of non-injury of others is not undertaken simply for the sake of others; it is for the opening of one's own heart as well. Without an attitude of ahimsa, one sees others as somehow less significant, less sentient than oneself. This is callousness, not love.

So mentally I took a vow not to injure any creature, at the very least while on my retreat, and if possible to continue thereafter.

After meditation, I laid out a plastic sheet and a blanket on a level spot near my cave's entrance and began my yoga practice. I was about to lie on my back to do a shoulder stand, when I glanced behind me. There, on my blanket, was a strange-looking creature basking in the sun. A closer look and I realized that it was a feisty, black scorpion. Another two seconds and I would have lain on him.

Determined to honor my vow of non-injury, I picked up a small stick and cautiously flicked the scorpion about 10 feet away. Hopefully that conveyed the message that I was in town and wanted my space.

A few minutes later, I felt something crawling up my pant leg. Remembering the scorpion, I quickly brushed whatever it was out of my pants. A large black ant rolled out of my pant leg, mortally injured. Carefully, I placed him in the grass in hopes that he might recover. I watched as he struggled to get up and walk. Within a minute, however, another large black ant found him, grappled with him for a few moments, overcame him, and carried him away. He was now food for his own kind. I had been the cause. Not a very good beginning to my vow of non-injury.

Continuing with asanas, a short time later, I discovered I had lain on another ant, injuring him as well. I could hardly believe it. I was an ahimsa disaster!

Placing him in the grass in hopes that he might recover, I watched as he struggled to stand. Clearly, he was not going to make it. Rather than see him suffer, only to be eaten alive, I took a stick and, with a sincere prayer for his soul, crushed him.

A worse beginning to my vow of non-injury could hardly be imagined. My heart ached for that ant, whose life I had snuffed. I felt such compassion for him, as if he were a close friend or loved one who had died. I prayed for him, aware that my sentiments would probably appear silly to any onlooker.

Then I recalled the love St. Francis of Assisi had shown for all creatures. He treated not only every creature, but nearly every*thing* as a dear brother or sister. Such a sense of communion with all creatures and things had previously seemed incomprehensible and unattainable to me. Only a saint could feel that way, I had assumed. Yet here I was, actually feeling compassion and brotherhood for an ant, no doubt thanks to all the hours of meditation, which must have heightened my spiritual sensibilities. Perhaps this attitude was not so silly; perhaps it is how we should live all the time.

Suddenly, I became aware of how I had previously lived so removed in my consciousness from nature. Absorbed in my human work, desires, aspirations, and relations, I could only view nature as entirely separate from myself. Without a thought, I had killed hundreds of ants invading our room in Kerala.* Indeed, a whole side of my personality—what now felt to me a crass, thoughtless side, concerned only with my own comfort—seemed manifestly opposed to this brotherhood with all creatures. If I could really observe this vow of ahimsa, that callous side of myself would necessarily disappear.

After yoga, as I walked through that beautiful Himalayan forest to town for my meal, I savored the transforming possibilities of maintaining a vow of ahimsa for the rest of my life. It would change me. I knew it. Yet how could I succeed? I had already failed miserably.

Then it came to me:

Love, not a mere vow, is the essence of ahimsa. Love and compassion for all is what uplifts the world. Ahimsa

---

* At the ashram of Ammachi, the "Hugging Saint." In India's tropics, invasions of incredibly intelligent ants are a part of daily life. They will find your food no matter how you hide it, lock it up, or hang it out of reach.

is a powerful expression of truth, a pure intention to develop care, awareness, and universal love that honors and respects all life. Nonetheless, it is the ego that makes a vow. How many tiny creatures did I unknowingly kill every time I walked to town? Unbounded love is the goal. Didn't St. Francis exemplify love, not vows?

After eating, bathing, and washing my clothes, I walked back towards my cave by a route that took me through the market. I wanted to buy a couple more bananas for dinner.

Gangotri's marketplace is lined on both sides by sadhus begging alms. I had passed that way many times, but had contributed only rarely, being hard-pressed for money myself. The sadhus did not hold it against me. Having gradually realized that I was not just a Western tourist but a serious sadhak, they greeted me with warm, bright smiles, saluted me with joined palms, and called out merrily, "Hari Om!" or sometimes, "Mauna Baba!"*

Their warmth was one of the wonderful charms of living in that community. Also, there was a strong bond of sharing a common goal; nearly everyone there, sadhak or pilgrim, was motivated by a sincere devotion to the Divine. This held true even for many of the shopkeepers, most of whom prominently displayed in their shop

---

* A term of respect addressed to a sadhak who observes a vow of silence for a long time.

a picture of the particular deity they worshipped or a photo of their guru.

Just as I turned off the main lane onto a walkway, I nearly bumped into someone. We looked up and recognized each other simultaneously. It was an Indian porter I had encountered several times before.

He immediately extended his arms and hugged me awkwardly, my face forcefully buried in his army jacket at his shoulder. As he released me, in a loud voice he asked, "Gaumukh? Tapovan?* Only 200 rupees a day. Come on! Gaumukh? You going?"

I cringed. Every time I ran into this fellow, he hugged me, then loudly offered his services to guide me further into the mountains (at an inflated price, I later discovered). The Swami at Krishnashram had seen one of our encounters and had warned me about the fellow. He told me that a Western woman, a previous client of this porter's, had taught him the many virtues a hug. He had apparently grasped that in the West, a hug endears two people forever, and this might be used to promote his business.

As far as I was concerned, this routine was getting old. I shook my head "No" and continued on my way.

That afternoon, while meditating in the sun at the brink of the canyon overlooking the Ganga, the thought of the porter arose. With it came irritation. The porter's hugs and the warmth of the sadhus might outwardly appear similar, yet they were worlds apart. The sadhus

---

* Gaumukh is the lower end of the glacier from which the Ganga flows, about 18 kilometers upstream from Gangotri. Tapovan is another point several hours' hike beyond Gaumukh. Pilgrims often hire guides to take them to these sacred spots.

wanted nothing of me; the porter's affection was clearly motivated by financial self-interest.

I imagined telling him off at length about his hypocritical hugs. Scathing rebukes revolved in my mind. Yet all the while, I knew my anger was fruitless. I would never bother to confront the porter. Why was my mind whirling on this?

I continued to meditate and felt myself slipping into a deep wholeness of awareness that seemed to embrace everything around me. The world seemed an abstraction, pervaded by that wholeness of my awareness. After a time, this wholeness was interrupted by a question: Why had I reacted so strongly to the porter?

I sat with it. It seemed to me my reaction was based on subconscious assumptions about what was appropriate and proper. It wasn't proper for the porter to repeatedly sell to me. It was low of him to use hugging as a sales technique. He came on far too strong. I was justified in feeling irritation. I was justified in rebuking him, in tearing into him—if I weren't in silence, that is.

That thought made me laugh. What a joke! What good was it to be in silence and meditating in a cave if this is how I thought?

This is not the way I want to be in the world. My reactivity contradicts everything I aspire towards. It diminishes me. Never mind being "spiritual"; I don't even feel gracious or kind.

My way of thinking, and my irritation gave me less equanimity and evenness than many mature, kind people I've known who have never meditated a day. I felt ashamed. How long have I had these assumptions? Who knows? For years, perhaps even since I was a child. And clearly, they are shaping me into a person I don't respect. It is time I let them go and find a new way.

As I continued to meditate, I had the thought, *if only I hadn't run into the porter today, I'd be having a peaceful meditation . . .*

Immediately, I caught myself. This was it! This was the cornerstone of my angry reaction: That my interaction with the porter was random, that he really needn't, or shouldn't be in my life; that he was merely a pest, an inconvenience disturbing my peaceful retreat—and this randomness allowed my anger to erupt. Whereas if I saw a purpose in him showing up, I could not be so dismissive.

My assumption that this porter has no business in my life is my own arrogance, pure and simple. Doesn't this deny the perfect intelligence within life, the flawless and purposeful arrangement of every event and person I encounter? Doesn't my anger ultimately arise from the attitude, "I only want to experience what I think is meaningful"? Wasn't I, in a sense, presuming to know more than the infinite intelligence of life, which kept arranging for me to bump into the porter?

Who was I to say my meeting the porter was meaningless and random? Was anything random? He was, after all, a perfect test of my patience, and he was certainly giving me the chance to work through my anger. Clearly, I *needed* him in order to gain self-awareness and grow as a person. Far from my bad luck, he was a gift.

Suddenly, I felt a wave of love for that porter, who was simply being who he was, earning a living the best way he could, innocently and perfectly performing his role. He had only reflected my own lack of love and understanding, and so gave me the gift of a clear opportunity to grow. He was not only a beautiful, unique human being, but also for me a perfect instrument—and for that I had condemned him! Once again, I felt humbled.

> *Love means loving all, just as it is, without feeling a need to change anything or anyone. This means seeing the perfection of each and every event, seeing the beauty of every person, such that you cannot but feel grateful, even when you are dealt what you would not have chosen.*

With this realization, my mind dropped into the peace of inner Being,[*] the stillness of pure awareness. As I sat in that unbounded peace and inner silence, shakti[†] filled my body more and more. A powerful feeling of buoyancy filled me.

But where is this surge of energy coming from?

Then something Mahatma Gandhi once said came to me.

> *"I have learnt through bitter experience the one supreme lesson to conserve my anger, and as heat conserved is transmuted into energy, even so our anger controlled can be transmuted into a power which can move the world."*[‡]

---

[*]   Transcendent pure Existence or pure Being is another term for pure awareness or the Infinite. When, in meditation, you transcend the faintest impulse of a thought, you transcend all activity. You are simply Being, abiding in a state of pure, unbounded awareness. In that state, there is no individuality, no activity, just eternal silence, infinite pure awareness left by itself.

[†]   Spiritual energy. See Glossary for a more in depth explanation.

[‡]   Easwaran, Eknath. *Gandhi The Man.* 2nd ed. Petaluma, CA: Blue Mountain Center of Meditation, Nilgiri Press, 1978: 74.

CHAPTER 5

Being in the Present

Watch a tree.
It knows how to be.

The next morning, I awoke before dawn and sat up in the darkness of my cave to meditate. After an hour or so, my awareness began steadily flowing at a more subtle level, more clearly, than it had since I had first arrived in Gangotri.

As I meditated in the darkness of my cave, the sensation quickly became one of floating in a celestial realm, in the sacred love and light of what could only be called Heaven. *The kingdom of heaven is within you . . .* How true were these words!

This was not just the peace and stillness of pure awareness, this was indescribable sweetness. It was sitting in the presence of the Divine, bathed in holy light and love. Never before had I dwelt in such a sublime and delicate level of pure feeling. Several hours passed like so many minutes.

Soon it was time to stop meditation, do asanas, and go to town for my meal. But I could not stop. I felt myself under the guidance of a divine autopilot, intent on traversing a heavenly abode of sublime feeling. How could I wrest control and force myself out of meditation just for the sake of a meal? I could only surrender. Indeed, it was clear that I was not even the one meditating; meditation was simply going on.

Forty minutes later, the meditation came to an end naturally, without my having to violate that inner flow of delicate feeling. Now, however, I would have to hurry through my asanas, for if I arrived even five minutes late to the annakshetra, I would miss my meal.

To my surprise, the divine autopilot wouldn't let go. Assuming the various yogic postures, I could not but hold each one until receiving the full benefit. To hurry would have felt crude and jarring. Again, I was not the one doing; as my mind had been held in a flow of grace before, so now my body was in that flow. Asanas were simply going on. Not only were they effortless, but this, clearly, was what asanas were meant to be—each position a self-contained prayer, suffusing body and mind with sublime felicity.

By the time I finished yogasanas, my last slim hope to catch my meal was to run the mile or so into town to make up for lost time. But again, I could not. The Divine continued to set the pace. Walking even slower than usual, I savored the sights of the forest around me, stopped to smell wild flowers, and enjoyed the sight of colorful bushes and views of the river. I just couldn't do otherwise. To rush and fail to enjoy that forest's exquisite beauty would have felt unforgivably crude. Giving up on my free meal, I resigned myself to buying something to eat, though it would probably be oily, over spiced, and overpriced.

Now, it struck me: For my whole life, I had been subtly hurrying, impatiently or anxiously wanting to speed things up, to get beyond what I was doing in the present, to whatever was next. This subtle impatience and hurry had dominated my life. I hurried asanas, hurried eating, hurried daily chores; in the States, I used to hurry to work, hurry at work, and then hurry home. It seemed to me that I must hurry more than most people. How ironic! About the only thing I didn't hurry was my meditation.

I had the feeling that my impatience to experience more must be, in a roundabout way, an impatience to realize oneness with the Divine, for only the Infinite could fully quench my thirst for more. Indeed, most of the time, I hurried so I would have time to meditate—or because I had spent so much time in meditation that I had to hurry to get everything else done. Now the irony of this struck me: How could I ever realize oneness with the Divine in such a state of frenzy?

> *To be hurried is to be out of the Now, out of one's Self. It is to be caught in the small ego, separate from, and discontent with the perfection of life as it is. The way to Be is to surrender to the pace life sets in this moment.*

> *The past is no more, and the future is yet a dream; there is only the Now. The Divine cannot be experienced in a nonexistent future towards which we hurry, but only right now, in this moment.*

With this, I felt a new freedom: How wonderful to simply Be, right now; not waiting for some future perfect state. How joyful, peaceful, and easy! How liberating to resist the

impulse of hurry and offer it into the flame of the Now.
Yes, sometimes God might set a quick pace; then I would
have to move and act efficiently. Yet this need not kill the
unmoved, inner silence and stillness of Being. Each act is
meditation when it proceeds at the pace of the Now.

*Realizing God is a matter of becoming more and more
patient, for what is perfect patience but love? That is,
unconditional love for this moment and everything in it.*

I approached the annakshetra. No one was to be seen.
The meal was finished.

I turned to head down the walk towards the shops
where I could buy some food, but in that moment, the
young Tibetan server emerged from the annakshetra's
small cooking hut. He held my meal on a tin plate, which
he offered to me with a broad smile.

His thoughtfulness overwhelmed me. With joined palms,
I saluted him, smiling in thanks. He blushed at my gratitude.

The Divine had set the pace of the morning and had
taken care of everything. My meal had been provided,
and my tardiness had even become the occasion of love
and goodwill.

*We don't have to think to be in the present,
We are in it.
Thinking is for the past and future;
This moment is beyond thought.*

Swami Dineshananda had invited me to see him as often as I wanted. But since moving into my cave, I had gone to his hermitage only once a week. Nonetheless, each time I sat with him, his bright countenance and the spiritual energy he emanated attracted me immensely.

Usually, I found Dineshananda alone. We would sit quietly; now and then he might say a few words and chuckle gently with a merry twinkle in his eyes. Inevitably, he would offer me food, and I always brought something for him. Despite this seemingly insignificant exchange, I felt tremendous grace flowing from him to me all the while. I never found my time with him boring or disappointing. That morning, after eating and bathing, I felt compelled to go and see Swami Dineshananda again.

As I neared his cave entrance, I saw that he was alone, lying on his bed reading one of the *Upanishads*.* Hearing me approach, he sat up and waved me in. Seated on his bed, with his smiling, bearded countenance, he looked like a happy, radiant, Indian gnome.

I entered his cave and sat cross-legged on the floor in front of him. I placed the fruit I had brought beside him. He handed me one of the bananas back and I ate it. Then he offered me some walnuts.

This was the first time I had been in his cave. It was entirely man-made. In fact, it was really a cement hut, perfectly clean and dry—a far more civilized affair than my rough-hewn hole under a boulder. Taking two walnuts in my right hand, I squeezed them against each other until one broke open—a trick I had learned as a child.

With a quizzical look on his face, Dineshananda picked up a single walnut and tried to do the same. He grimaced

---

* Important Indian scriptures dealing with ultimate truth. See Glossary.

with effort, but the nut held its own. Smiling, he handed it to me. I broke the nut open for him, showing him the trick. He chuckled. Then he offered me more food and tastes of several Ayurvedic* medicines, which he mimed—by pointing to his well-nourished stomach—were good for digestion.

After eating these and various other treats, we went outside and sat in the sun. Soon the translator came. I wrote a note to Dineshananda saying how I felt drawn to staying in the holy air around him. The translator read it to him in Hindi. Dineshananda laughed and replied in a few words.

"That holiness is not in any one place," came the translation, "one must live in that spiritual power wherever one is."

Yes, this must be true, and it was what I hoped to someday always experience for myself. His words reassured me that he understood the reason for the infrequency of my visits: Through dedication to my spiritual practices, I was attempting to rise to a state of permanently living in that spiritual energy.

This is something I had learned from being with Amma. When people first meet her, the temptation is to strive to be in her physical presence as much as possible. It feels so good to be in the presence of a saint. Indeed, for a time this may be extremely beneficial. But ultimately, she expects people to go within and find their own power—not the power of the ego, but of the divine Self that dwells within us all. That is the only way to realize the Self. You don't realize your divine Self in someone else.

---

*   Ayurveda is India's ancient traditional medical science.

Dineshananda said a few words to the translator, who got up and went into the cave. A moment later he returned with a paper, which he gave to me. As I took the paper, the translator told me that it was an English translation of a poem that Dineshananda had written in Hindi. While I silently read the poem, Dineshananda smiled brightly. It beautifully and succinctly expressed various aspects of Dineshananda's realization of his own Self as the universal, omnipresent, divine Being.[*]

Having on a previous visit told him that I might someday write something about my experiences in the Himalayas, I now asked Dineshananda through another note if I might reprint his poem.

"Yes," he answered in English. Then he brought out a handwritten sheet with some changes to the translation. He asked me to check that all the changes were correct and included on the version he had first given me. As I did this, a few other devotees joined us, and Dinesha began an animated conversation with them. A few minutes later, I quietly slipped away and went to the "meditation room."

As I entered the tiny stick hut, I saw that it had been cleaned and reinforced, probably for my benefit, as I had never seen anyone else use it. That Dineshananda would have done this for me made me appreciate his quiet sweetness and thoughtfulness all the more.

Upon closing my eyes, my mind was immediately sunk in a blissful expanse. Not only my mind, but even my body—every atom of my being—seemed to dissolve into That, as if I had become all of space, galaxies teeming within me. At the same time, shakti, spiritual energy, tangibly filled my body. Such a meditation could only have been the result of sitting with Dineshananda for that hour

---

[*] See *Song of Me,* by Swami Dineshanandaji, on page 223.

or so. I had felt the same quality before, while meditating in Amma's presence.

Continuing to meditate, a question arose in my mind: *How will the spiritual energy I experience here in the Himalayas possibly be maintained once I leave?* As soon as this question arose, an answer came:

Be in the present.

In that moment, this seemed the key to everything. By being in the present, no energy would be wasted on superfluous thoughts, desires, and activities; there would be no loss of spiritual energy. It would naturally remain constant and undiminished. Whereas when we live immersed in thoughts of what has been or what is yet to come, we are losing energy every moment, with each thought.

To Be is to have only one thought: simple, full awareness of this moment. That is the equivalent of no thought, of no mind. By contrast, the active mind is nothing other than awareness continually broken into countless thoughts pertaining to past and future.

I was reminded of a conversation I had years ago with a physicist who was also a teacher of meditation. He had compared the ordinary mind to ordinary white light, and the mind of a Self-realized person to the light of a laser. Whereas ordinary white light is a jumble of many different wavelengths of light, laser light is one pure wavelength, with all the individual wavelengths aligned into one, coherent wave. Ordinary mind is a jumble of many thoughts, whereas an enlightened mind is pure mind—coherent, whole, unbroken awareness.

Certainly, many people experience glimpses of this even before enlightenment. The tennis pro who reacts to make an impossible return, or an Olympic skier who finds his body moving perfectly in a split second to make a gate. In such moments, there can be no thought of past and future; there is hardly a mind at all, just fully present awareness, fully engaged. There is both inner silence and spontaneous, outer dynamism—and the peak of precision in action. This is a state of optimal performance and enjoyment that psychologists have referred to as a state of "flow."*

Yet for even the greatest athlete, that state of being fully present is temporary. The athlete may feel grace during their event or performance, but then in everyday life, it is gone. If, however, a person can learn to be in this moment, every moment, without break, their life will always move in that power and grace of the Now. They will always be in a state of flow. This seemed to me a fuller meaning than I had previously understood of Dineshananda's statement, "One must live in that spiritual power wherever one is."

As I sat in that unbounded state, another question arose. It is said that God is Love, and both my Christian upbringing and Amma placed much emphasis on love. What is the relationship between the state of simple Being and love?

An answer came:

Being is the foundation of love. How can I love another while distracted by thoughts of past or future? I love only to the extent I am present. To be fully present means that my full awareness, unconcerned with my own ego, is given to this moment. The feeling associated with

---

* See *Flow: The Psychology of Optimal Experience,* by Mihaly Csikszentmihalyi, 1990, New York: Harper and Row. ISBN 0-06-092043-2 *this selfless attention is love—for whatever or whoever I am with in that moment.*

I was reminded of my meditation that morning. I had felt fully present to my own experience, and dwelt in a heavenly realm filled with the sweetness of love. When I was fully present with nature walking to town, I felt awe and love for nature. When I am fully present with another person, I feel overflowing love for them. Full presence equals full love.

What makes this selfless attention possible? Delight. It is blissful to be fully present, to perceive the divine Essence of what or who is before you. This is Essence (you) perceiving Essence (in another). A union of Love made possible by presence.

After my meditation, I slipped out of Dineshananda's hermitage and returned to my cave. Recording these insights in my journal, I felt a faint intention arise regarding the future of that writing: *Perhaps these insights will be included in a future book . . .*

Suddenly my mind, which had been quiet before, began to bubble with excitement. For the first time that day, the divine autopilot disappeared. In an instant, my attachment had drawn a veil over the present moment.

Being is infinitely powerful, yet so delicate—with even the faintest attachment, we are cast from that heavenly state. No wonder the divine Essence of life remains invisible to most of us. No wonder we suffer disharmony in our lives, for the human mind ever abounds with desires, aspirations, hopes, and dreams. How rare, amidst this flurry of attachment, to discover the most precious secret of desireless Being, fulfilled in Itself.

There is no greater victory for the soul
Than to banish thought of past and future.

The next day, as I bathed in the Ganga after my meal, Philippe came walking towards me from town, beaming his usual friendly smile. He had a large backpack on. When he reached me, he told me he was catching a bus to Uttarkashi and then to Rishikesh and would not be back. The cold and increasing rain were getting to him; after two months in Gangotri, he yearned for warmth. We traded addresses as I walked him to the bus stand. The bus driver boarded, Philippe and I hugged, and he climbed onto the bus. A few minutes later, it drove away. My first friend, my best friend in Gangotri, was now gone.

I felt sad at Philippe's departure. It had been weeks since I had given a single thought to leaving. But now, after returning to my cave, my mind teemed with restless thoughts of going. Life in a cave was cold, difficult, and lonely. Lately it had been raining often; gone were the days of blissful walks in the sun. I often bathed in the freezing Ganga in the rain, then walked to my cave in a downpour. Since the cave was so cold, and I had little warm clothing or bedding, I didn't warm up until the next morning—if it happened to be sunny.

Even that very moment, as I contemplated leaving, ominous storm clouds loomed in the western sky over the mountains. Comfort, warmth, and plenty of good food were only a six-hour bus ride away in Uttarkashi. I could pack in less than an hour and catch a bus that afternoon. It sounded good, very good . . .

The urge to leave grew until it cried out from every cell of my being. I forced myself to resist it: What of the bliss and deep meditations I had been enjoying? How could I leave Gangotri now? Wasn't this desire to leave just a purging of attachments, stirred by powerful meditations and Philippe's departure? *Control yourself, Ajayan!* Sitting on my meditation blanket, I closed my eyes while my mind whirled with thoughts of leaving like a dervish gone mad.

I knew from past experience that intensive meditation could uproot deep mental and emotional attachments, aversions, reactions, neuroses, and fears. This was a necessary purging to free you from the conditioning of past experience, so you could live in the unconditioned Peace of Being. The key was to remain indifferent to all thoughts during such purification, neither resisting them nor giving them credence. How many countless new meditators had I helped through the siren song of thoughts in meditation? Yet now that same song was irresistibly luring me to the comfort and warmth of Uttar Kashi and Rishikesh.

For more than an hour, this excruciating inner struggle raged inside me. Then gradually, from beneath the turmoil of thoughts, a faint new light emerged.

I have slipped out of the Now and into thoughts of past and future comforts. When all is said and done, isn't this the source of my turmoil? To leave Gangotri now would be to fail, utterly. It is not time to go, not at all. My inner work is far from finished; my retreat here is the opportunity of a lifetime.

With this, calm and clarity dawned. I picked up my journal and wrote:

No one can realize the state of Being so long as they remain a slave of the mind. You are not the mind that flits about on thoughts. Stay in the dignity of the Self. Watch the mind and its movements, feel whether your mind is in harmony with the subtle stream of life or is in discord with that ease and peace. That much is usually obvious. Then you will know what to do, or at least you will know to stay in the unknown.

To observe the mind, to resist being caught by its wiles, is the essence of heroism (and sanity) on the spiritual path.

Still, in the back of my mind, a question remained: Was I up to it? I was not leaving today, but how long could I last? How far could I take this?

CHAPTER 6

Austerity

To sit in divine consciousness is to abide in the heart of all religions—in divine love, in Christ's consciousness, in the Truth Buddha and Shankara realized, in the holiest of holy, the fountainhead of life, in the one God of all faiths.

The weather continued to turn for the worse. As a result, I spent more and more time inside my cave and less outside. My practice grew in intensity; the cave walls reflected the energy of meditation, creating a concentrated atmosphere of silence and shakti (spiritual energy). Just to sit and close my eyes was enough for my mind to dissolve into pure consciousness. Experiences of many flavors of the Divine came: divine love, light, bliss, the pervasive vastness of the Self—but with these, inner pain as well.

This pain was not unfamiliar to me. It was due not only to the cold and discomfort of cave living, but to a subtle, sometimes agonizing process of inner purification stirred by long meditation. Over the years, while on retreats, I had often experienced an intense, inner baking, as if I were sitting in an oven or suffering from a case of the flu. Sometimes I would feel emotional anguish in my chest, or a piercing anguish of soul that seemed subtler and deeper than ordinary emotion. Often these experiences were so intense that to continue meditating became almost unbearable. Some might call this a healing crisis; only in this case, the healing was metaphysical as well as physical.

The good news was that such experiences were inevitably followed by greater bliss, expansiveness, spiritual energy, and clarity, in and out of meditation. To the extent of the pain of purification, a sense of grace and tangible personal transformation followed. I never had any doubts that the pain was worth it, to feel the deep peace and presence of the Divine, one's body filled with felicity and healing energy, one's mind expanded and renewed in wonder for life, and one's heart opened. Sometimes, after such a meditation, I felt like a newborn child. If I could share any one thing with others in my lifetime, it would be this experience of transformation from within by pure Spirit. It was why I had been so passionate about teaching meditation since the early 70's.

So, meditating in my cave on those cold and rainy days, I usually welcomed those sensations of self-sacrifice in the fires of purification. As the days passed, however, and the purification intensified, I sometimes wondered how much more I could bear.

Often the thought came to abandon my cave that very day, to hop out of meditation, pack, and leave Gangotri. Yet I forced myself to sit and endure, though this felt about as blissful as forcing myself to hard physical labor with a fever. Then the inner clouds would clear, for a meditation or for a day, divine bliss would flood my being, and all thoughts of leaving would vanish like morning mist dispersed by the sun.

It helped knowing that such purification had been experienced by contemplatives of many of the world's spiritual traditions. This, in fact, was the meaning of *tapas* (spiritual practices performed intensely and in a spirit of self-denial). India's traditional texts declare tapas to play an important role in spiritual development. It is said to produce a subtle heat that burns away a person's impurities, gradually endowing him or her with radiant spiritual energy as the veils of dross obscuring the innermost Self dissolve.

In the Christian tradition, St. John of the Cross wrote *The Ascent of Mt. Carmel* and *The Dark Night of the Soul* to encourage monks and nuns in his spiritual care who were suffering the pangs of purification on their contemplative path. He compared the soul in contemplation to a piece of wood burning in a fire. God's love, the purifying fire, though all light and divine joy, is experienced as intense pain to the unrefined, impure soul. Yet only by undergoing that pain of purification is the soul transformed into the likeness of the divine fire that devours it. It is a wonderfully apt and insightful metaphor.

Nonetheless, austerity should not be taken too far. St. Francis of Assisi, I had heard, referred to his body as "brother ass," and subjected himself to intense austerities, from which his health suffered. As he was dying, he purportedly expressed that perhaps he should not have been so hard on his body. With the increasing cold and rain, and my meager, imbalanced diet, my physical stamina and vitality had noticeably waned. In the name of prudence, I decided to periodically supplement my meal with some vegetables at a cafe.

During one such meal, as I sat at an outdoor table overlooking the Ganga while eating a bowl of potato curry, something caught my eye. A tall, bearded, blond-haired Western man, dressed in the orange dhoti and shawl of a Swami, was buying cookies at a nearby shop. He was arguing loudly with the shopkeeper, apparently over the price of the cookies.

As he completed his transaction and turned around, our eyes met. I smiled, in part as a gesture of friendliness, and partly because I sympathized with his efforts to renegotiate the price of cookies. Gangotri shop owners routinely added twenty percent to the list price of every item, as it cost them extra to bring goods to this remote location. Smiling in return, he walked towards me as he opened his snack.

Once he was closer, I saw that his orange robes and brown, wool ski cap were tattered and dirty. His hair, reaching well below his shoulders, was unkempt. He seemed to be a Western sadhu.

"Hari Om," he said as he reached my table. "Mind if I join you?" His accent was hard to place, but I thought it might be Italian.

I invited him to sit by motioning to a chair, then mimed that I was in silence by zipping my mouth shut.

"Oh, you're in silence. Fine. Okay if I talk to you?" he asked.

I nodded my head in assent, welcoming his conversation with a gesture of my hands. Then, with hardly a moment's hesitation, he began a monologue unlike any I have ever heard.

"I don't know about you," he began, "because we just met, but for me there is nowhere else. I'm going to spend the rest of my life here, doing *sa-dha-na.*" He emphasized the word "sadhana," as if it were something mysterious, and gave me a knowing look.

He offered me a cookie, and added apologetically, "I don't usually eat these, but four years of ashram food has ruined my stomach." His tone became angry. "I don't know why they make it so hot. It's poison! Food should be medicine. When I cook for myself, I cook *med-i-cine*. Yes, medicine," he repeated, nodding serenely.

I couldn't agree more. Indian ashram food was often abundantly laced with chilies. I had wondered what the attraction was in experiencing severe pain while eating.

"But we shouldn't need food at all, really," he continued. "Look at those pines; they just sip a little water. They don't need anything else. That's enough for them. But they don't *do* much either. That's how I'm going to live— without eating." His clear, blue eyes flashed with excitement and intrigue, as he studied my face for a response.

"Yes, I'll wean myself from food," he continued dramatically. "Maybe just eat pine needles. I've tried a few, you know. I felt they were promising. But I'll have to stop moving around; I'll have to follow *their* example." With a sweeping motion of his hand, he indicated the pine trees on the mountains around us.

"I'll start by just eating herbs," he added in a calmer tone. "There are enough herbs in these mountains to keep you alive, you can be sure of that. A friend of mine in Delhi said he would teach me which herbs to eat. In fact, he'd give me all the herbs I need." He surveyed the river thoughtfully for a few moments. "Yes, I think he'd do that," he said, nodding.

Now he turned to address me. "I'm also weaning myself from cloth, you know. These," he said, as he tugged at his shawl, "we don't need these. At least we shouldn't. I'm going to spend my winters here, and I can't see how that's possible, except by gradually reducing the need for cloth."

His logic escaped me. I wobbled my head gently sideways in Indian fashion. This was a wonderfully ambiguous gesture that usually meant, "yes," "okay," or "I agree with you, you are absolutely right." But it could also mean a less definite, "maybe so," or even, "I'm wobbling my head 'yes,' but I really don't think so; I'm just being polite to spare your feelings." It was up to the other person to correctly interpret your wobble. During this conversation, I found myself wobbling a great deal.

"Then there's sleep," he continued. His eyes flashed and his nostrils flared with determination, as he inhaled deeply. "Sleep shouldn't be necessary. I've begun to reduce sleep, but it's hard. I'm down to 7 hours, but that's still too much," he said, shaking his head slowly, "waaay too much. If I find the right place here—you need the right place, you know, a place that has the right energy, a beauty that moves you—then I won't need to sleep."

Thoughtfully, he surveyed the mountains for a few moments and said, "Of course you can't do much without food, sleep, and cloth. You stay in one place. I suppose I'll even stop yogasanas and just meditate, but meditation doesn't keep the body fit." He turned to me and continued. "That's why I like asanas. I've been working at them. You might say I'm at the intermediate level. I go slowly. A Swami watched me once and told me I move like a snail, but that's the idea as far as I'm concerned. I'll master them before long, and then I'll stop even those." Again his eyes flashed as he scrutinized me for my reaction.

By this time, I really wanted to get to my bath and laundry, but it was hard to gracefully extract myself from his conversation. I became alert to pounce on the first opportunity.

"I haven't decided if I will give up the scriptures," he continued. "There's the *Gita*. I like that. That got me started. I *got* the Atman and that really . . ."

Wobbling my head in Indian fashion, I stood up and saluted him with folded palms. Then I showed him my laundry and waved in the direction of the river.

"Oh, you've got to go. Where're you staying?" he asked.

I didn't really want him to know about my cave, so I vaguely waved in the general direction of it.

"The Tourist Guest House?" he asked.

I shook my head no, made a rounded gesture with my hands and silently mouthed, "guha."

"Ah, a guha? You're in a cave?" he said, surprised. "I'm looking for a cave too."

I took out a notepad and pen and wrote a note to him.

He read it aloud over my shoulder as I wrote it: "'Wish-you-the-best-of-luck.' Right," he said. "Same to you."

I smiled, saluted again, and mouthed, "Hari Om."

"Hari Om," he replied.

This fellow may have been obnoxious and maybe even crazy, yet he possessed an innocence and sincerity I could not help but appreciate. Still, I would not be disappointed if our paths did not cross again.

Solitude may yield unexpected riches, like your Self.

For the entire next week, the cold and rain continued, and my tapas was fast losing its appeal. There was such spiritual energy in my body that the first hour of each meditation was crystalline pure consciousness—an unbounded, gleaming jewel of divinity, blissfully shining in my heart or in my forehead. The rest of the four or five hours of each sitting was unbearable torture—heat, every cell aching as if I had the flu, and occasional pangs of emotional anguish. My body was being assailed from without by the cold and wet, and from within by the fire of intense purification.

I could hardly remember the sunny days I had spent in blissful communion with nature. I had been in my cave a little over four weeks. It seemed to me that I had never been warm, never seen the sun, never enjoyed any beauty there. I had lived in Seattle for many years, and this was very much like the worst of a Seattle winter: constant and dreary rain, clouds, and cold. Only now I was not living in a comfortable home, but in a dank hole under a big rock in the forest.

Sitting in meditation one morning, mentally bemoaning my suffering, I decided that I would leave the very next day. *What more is there for me in Gangotri in this freezing cave? Maybe I can rough it out for another few days, maybe even for a couple of torturous weeks more, but how much deeper would I go? I want to Be with family and friends, Be while I write, Be while I teach. I don't want to just be on an eternal retreat. I have to leave!*

The siren call of thought had caught me firmly in its grip. Or perhaps it was simply good sense. I hoped the latter. That afternoon I made the rounds to say my goodbyes. First I went to see Krishnadas. He and his buddy Swami were now living on a porch outside a rustic ashram near a large waterfall. This waterfall was known as Gauri Kund. It is said that here is where the Ganga first descended onto the earth from the heavens. (After its crushing intensity was broken by Shiva's* head; otherwise it would have destroyed the earth.) So close to the waterfall was their abode that Krishnadas had hung a blanket from the ashram's roof to shield their bedding from the waterfall's spray.

---

* Lord Shiva, destroyer and transformer, is one of the 3 main Hindu deities, along with Brahma and Vishnu.

They were sitting in front of an open fire, making tea. As I approached, Krishnadas rose with a broad smile.

"Hari Om," he boomed. He motioned for me to sit on a log placed on the porch. "Tea?" he asked.

Ordinarily, I didn't drink tea, the national beverage of India, because it kept me awake at night. But to be polite, I had a cup with them.

A large burlap bag of beans sat at our feet on the porch. This was unusual; a sadhu would not normally have such supplies. I nodded towards it and gave a questioning look.

"Family sent," Krishnadas replied.

Ah, so, he *was* in touch with his family, and they were at least in good enough shape financially to support him. I felt relieved. I would have hated to think my friend had left his family in poverty.

Pointing to my chest, then walking my fingers in the air in the direction of Uttarkashi, I mimed that I was leaving Gangotri.

Krishnadas nodded. "Uh, go to Uttarkashi sometimes, yes."

I shook my head and again mimed my departure. This time they understood.

"Come back soon?" Krishnadas asked.

I shook my head no. Then mimed that I needed to return to my home, family, and teacher. It took a few tries, but finally they understood.

"Okay. You go and then come back and we . . . uh, be sadhana brothers. I your sadhana good luck," said Krishnadas. I figured this comment referred to his having helped me find the cave. I could only smile and appreciate his love.

We munched on sweets for a few minutes; then a third Swami joined us. He was younger and spoke perfect English.

Krishnadas and his inseparable buddy began to talk to him about me. The newcomer translated.

"Even though you come from another country, we are your spiritual brothers. You are a serious sadhak. We invite you to come and stay with us."

Placing my hand over my heart, I smiled in appreciation. Nevertheless, I still had a family. "Perhaps I will return next year," I scribbled in a notepad and showed it to the English-speaking Swami, who translated.

Saluting them all, and drinking the love that shone in their eyes, I stood up to leave. Now I had to see Dineshananda.

As I approached Dineshananda's hermitage, I saw his diminutive, dark naked form seated outside his cave on a sheepskin. He was taking advantage of a sunny break in the clouds. He spotted me, broke into a broad smile, and waved me over. I sat in front of him on a wool mat, and we made the usual exchange of goodies; I handed him some sweets I had brought, and he offered me some pistachio nuts. As we snacked, Kishore, an extremely radiant, middle-aged disciple of Dineshananda who was visiting from Rajasthan, joined us. He spoke excellent English.

In Dineshananda's presence, I now wondered whether the whole idea of leaving might be just a form of mental purification. Perhaps I should really stay after all. I took out my notebook and pen and scribbled a note for Kishore to translate.

"I was feeling to leave tomorrow, but when I see you, I'm not sure. What does Swamiji feel about it?"

Dineshananda said a few words in a serious tone.

Kishore translated: "There is no coming or going. Wherever you go, I am there."

This may have been a profound response. In my present state of mind, though, it seemed vague and unsatisfactory.

It left the decision up to me. I had hoped for some clear-cut, divine guidance. Still, I was used to such hazy comebacks, as Amma was an absolute master of them. I had long ago concluded that she wanted me to find my answers within myself, and it looked like Dineshananda was of the same bent. Well, so be it. Truth is, in the final analysis, I usually did what I wanted anyway . . .

I also had one other piece of business on my mind: By now I was pretty sure I would include some of my Gangotri experiences in a book, and I might wish to include Dinesha's poem. I realized that a publisher would require written permission from Dinesha to reprint his poem. As awkward as it seemed to ask a saint living in the Himalayas without a stitch on his body for a legal agreement, what could I do?

Again I scribbled my question, "To reprint your poem I will need your written permission. Is that all right?"

Dineshananda smiled graciously, "Yes."

I handed him a brief permission agreement that I had made up in my cave, and after the translator read it to him, he signed it with great flourish.

"When I meditate," I wrote, "I clearly experience pure consciousness; what must I do to maintain that experience with eyes open?"

Again, he gave a serious reply: "You may experience all light, or all darkness, but continue to meditate until there is no identification with the body. That is the limit. Then you know the Self. Also, in meditation, forget all forms; eliminate all forms from the mind. That is the goal. Remember this principle."

This time his answer went straight to my heart. For most people, Amma recommends meditating on the form of one's beloved deity; for example, meditating on Krishna, Shiva, Christ, or Mary. Amma, as far as I knew, had always played down the idea of meditating directly

on the formless Infinite. Yet like a bee to a fragrant flower, my own mind was strongly drawn to the Infinite, which I had first experienced so vividly as a high-school student. That experience had made an indelible impression, and I simply could not help but be drawn towards That.*
That my own, natural inclination seemed other than that favored by Amma (though I felt her unspoken support) had once been a point of some dissonance for me. Now Dineshananda's answer was comforting and affirmed what I already knew in my heart.

> *There is no one way, or best way, to the divine Self. We must find the way suited to our own individual disposition, to our own unique strengths. Our path towards the Divine becomes joyful, and our progress rapid, only once we find the path that is uniquely our own.*

Dineshananda smiled at me with love in his eyes. He said a few words and Kishore translated, "Did you have any other questions?"

Appreciating anew Dineshananda's sweetness in validating my path of meditating on the formless Infinite, and feeling encouraged that he seemed so willing to answer my questions, I decided to take full advantage of the opportunity and ask him every important, unanswered question in my life.

I wrote in my notebook, "I enjoy my writing, and I try to offer it to God without attachment. Is it good for me to continue writing, or is writing an obstacle to my growth?"

Kishore translated and Dineshananda answered: "The words you write come from the heart. Write in such a

---

*   I've related this experience in the Introduction to this book.

way that the writing rubs the heart clean. Rub the heart clear of all words. When you have done that, you will find the perfect peace. Then there is nothing that need be done. Until you have that perfect peace, continue to write.

"Remember, the Self is the goal. Everything should be directed to That. You are here for the Self. You came for the Self, not for family or friends. Always live that way, even when with family and friends. Be detached while you do all your duties. Don't withdraw from life, just keep that detachment."

Again, his words were a supportive, healing balm for my heart. I quickly scribbled another question: "Living in the ashram is very busy—lots of people. I like the peace and solitude here. What does Swami feel about ashram life?"

"You can find peace even in the midst of people. Find that peace in yourself and it won't matter where you are. Here, people may get attached to the trees and mountains. They won't have that detachment and inner peace. Find it in yourself and you can be anywhere. Due to past actions, in past lives, you have to be in that ashram; you will be drawn there no matter what. Even if you try to leave, you will be forcibly drawn back. But where we are doesn't matter. Do your duties with detachment."

Again his answer brought peace. With folded hands, I bowed to him in gratitude. "Om Namah Shivayah."

"Now you have received all you came for," he said through the translator.

I nodded.

"Here the atoms are enlivened by the devotion of many saints," added Dineshananda. "So if one comes already a little enlightened, one will feel a much greater enlightenment. But wherever you go, I am there. Will you write about the Himalayas in your book?"

I nodded with enthusiasm.

He broke into a broad, radiant smile. Clearly, he was pleased.

"I will miss seeing your form," I wrote, "but I will come back someday."

"You are welcome anytime," he said. "Please come visit again. Kishore will answer any problem or question you have. Just write to him. When your book is published, send one to him and he will bring it to me."

"This is a great gift," I wrote, referring to the access to Kishore. "Thank you."

"The father places the child on his shoulder; then the child can see farther than the father," Dineshananda replied, referring to Kishore's ability to answer any question I might ask.

Now Kishore addressed me of his own accord. "I like spiritual people like you," he said. "And you have discovered a great secret: We dissipate so much energy by talking. Taking silence is good. But another way we lose energy is by eating. Fasting is also very good. There are beings up there," he said, pointing upstream, "that you can't see. They are just sitting in meditation. You can see them if you fast for at least seven days. I have seen them."

I nodded and smiled. Both Dineshananda and Kishore gazed deeply into my eyes with love. For perhaps thirty seconds, we were united in a timeless peace. Finally, I saluted them with joined palms, rose, put on my shoes, and walked back to my cave.

That night I packed, intending to catch an early bus the next morning to Uttarkashi. After blowing out the candles, I wrapped myself in my wool blankets and began to meditate before going to sleep. Instantly, I fell into the deepest experience of pristine, divine consciousness. I was absorbed in that crystalline ocean of bliss and divine light for perhaps an hour.

By the time I emerged from that state, one thing was certain: I wasn't going anywhere. Not yet. *How could I have even dreamt of leaving?! I have to stay.*

Suddenly, it seemed that the whole episode of wanting to leave had been a test of recognizing and rising above my attachments. Attached to my body, I had wanted to go because of the cold. Attached to my family and friends, I had wanted to leave because I missed them. Attached to the beauty of nature, it had also seemed time to go, since that beauty had receded with the onset of near constant rain and clouds. Attached to my writing, I had felt excited to get back to my computer and record what I had experienced here. Yet as Dineshananda had said to me, I had not come to Gangotri for any of these reasons. I came seeking the Divine, seeking to become at long last established in the Self. That work was just beginning.

It seemed to me that Dineshananda must have subtly planted the seed of this reversal of decision with his answers. It had sprouted in my meditation. Whether he had or not, I felt renewed determination.

To achieve success in the world—for instance in a career, as a performer, or in sports—requires great dedication. How much more so realizing the final Goal of all existence? What dedication and one-pointedness must that require? One must be willing to let go of everything, to pursue only the Highest, at whatever cost and sacrifice.

At this, I recalled something one of my favorite Christian saints, St. Teresa of Avila, had written:

They must have a great and very resolute determination to persevere until reaching the end, come what may, happen what may, whatever work is involved, whatever *criticism arises, whether they arrive or whether they die on the road, or even if they don't have courage for the trials that are met, or if the whole world collapses.* [*]

---

[*] St. Teresa of Avila. The Collected Works of St. Teresa of Avila, Volume II. Trans. Kieran Kavanaugh and Otilio Rodriguez. Washington, D.C.: Washington Province of Discalced Carmelites, ICS Publications, 1979: 117.

CHAPTER 7

Dance of Being

Never mind what is past or what is yet to come. This present moment is so exquisite, it requires your full attention.

I had just closed my eyes to begin afternoon meditation when I heard the crunch of footsteps on the rocks outside my cave. A moment later, two men I had never seen before crouched down and peered in. Greeting me with joined palms, they called out, "Hari Om!"

I was amazed at their timing. *My meditation schedule must be posted in Gangotri!*

I recognized my irritation was inappropriate, a symptom of attachment to my routine. After all, wasn't I here to learn to overcome such attachments, to learn to surrender to the will of the Divine? Clearly, I had a long ways to go . . .

Returning their salute, I waved them in.

One was in his late 60's. His thinning, shaggy gray hair, several days' stubble of a silver beard, a beat-up wool jacket, and old wool slacks gave him the look of a beggar. But his face was bright, serene, and friendly. The other, in his late thirties perhaps, with long, black hair and a full beard, was dressed in the orange dhoti and shawl of a Swami. He struck me as a bit stiff and formal and perhaps proud.

I smiled in greeting, mimed that I was in silence by zipping my mouth shut, and motioned for them to sit. For at least a full minute, we just sat quietly. Unfortunately, I had no food to offer, a major faux pas on my part. This made the silence uncomfortable, for me at least. I made a mental note to purchase some snacks for future visitors.

The old man looked around the cave, evaluating it with an impressed expression on his face. Finally, he broke the silence. "Shanti! Shanti!" (Peace! Peace!) he said in an enthusiastic, gravelly half-whisper. "Shanti! Shanti! Very good!" he repeated. Putting his hand on his heart, he sighed as he continued looking around the cave, then closed his eyes as if in blissful contemplation.

While the old man sat this way, the younger man asked me, "Do you know who this is?"

I shook my head.

"The vice-president of the Gangotri Temple Committee. He's a very simple man." He paused to allow me to digest this information. "Where are you from?"

I traced the letters USA in the air.

"Ah, American," he said.

I nodded, then showed them Amma's picture, hoping this would let them know that I was living with Amma in southern India.

"Your guru?" the young man asked.

I nodded again.

The old man took the picture, held it reverently before his face, and closed his eyes. Then he opened his eyes and held the picture to his heart. "Very good," he whispered. After a few moments of silence, he got up to leave. I decided it would be respectful to touch his feet, but before I could, he quickly lifted me and gave me a heartfelt hug. Then they both walked out of the cave, the Swami following. As they walked away, I heard the old man tell the Swami that I was a "true sadhak."

Continuing to meditate, I chided myself first for my irritation at their arrival, and secondly for not having any food to give them. Then a few moments later, I suddenly felt aware of an intense lack within myself.

Here I had been graced with so much inner spiritual experience; yet, clearly my development as a person lagged far behind my inner experience. I should have been so much more welcoming, so much more thoughtful and prepared to be a gracious host to visitors. Wasn't this a glaring contradiction? To be so blessed with daily experience of the Infinite, and then to fail to even embody the kindness and generosity of spirit that I'd seen in others? There was no way this could end well.

The personality must grow in concert with the spirit. Inner and outer must grow together.

This seemed to me a self-evident truth. I *knew* that to even begin to deserve what I'd been given, I had to dedicate myself to becoming an integrated human being— as if my life depended on it. Otherwise, all my spiritual practice was simply a form of pleasure seeking.

Their visit had been a humbling gift. The old man's appreciative comments affirmed my decision to stay in Gangotri. Yet his comments highlighted his graciousness and my own need for integration. It seemed to me the

Divine had come to me disguised as the old man to bring me this lesson.

We never know how the Divine will speak to us. A beggar, a Swami, an ant, a flower—all is God in disguise.

The words of Christ echoed in my mind: "Truly I tell you, whatever you did for one of the least of these brothers and sisters of mine, you did for me."[*]

The next morning, I awoke with a head cold and a slight earache. Up to that point, I had been lucky enough to maintain more or less good health. Other than a stomachache now and then, and losing a good deal of weight, I had been feeling as fit as ever. I could only hope this head cold would not develop further, since I had to remain healthy enough to walk to town for my meals and to get water, which I filtered from the river. A prolonged flu bug, keeping me stuck in the cave, could spell disaster.

As I began to meditate, I remembered what day it was: July 4th, my eldest daughter's 16th birthday. There were no phones in Gangotri, so I could not call her. All I could do was to wish her a happy birthday in my meditation. To compensate for my inability to tangibly wish my daughter a happy birthday, I spent a good portion of my meditation streaming happy birthday wishes to her in the form of healing energy. It seemed to me that I really

---

[*]   Matthew 25:40

connected with her and that she must be feeling some positive effect.

A couple of hours into my meditation, I felt something crawling at the base of my neck inside my clothes. Reaching under the neck of my sweater with my hand, I grabbed it—carefully so as not to crush whatever it was. When I opened my hand, I saw that it was a huge, black beetle. I gently placed it outside the cave.

As I continued meditating, though, I couldn't shake the thought that I had seen a beetle of this sort before. Where had it been? Wasn't it in a movie about Richard Burton's and John Speke's search for the source of the Nile? Their beetle, if I recalled correctly, crawled into Speke's ear while he slept—for the purpose of burrowing into his brain. Speke had stabbed the critter while it was still in his ear, and this had permanently damaged his hearing.[*]

The more I meditated on the beetle, the more afraid I became that it was indeed related to Speke's. This beetle had, after all, been heading in the direction of my ear, and my cave was infested with them—dreaded, black, Himalayan, brain-burrowing beetles!

After finishing meditation, I walked to town for my meal. The previous day I had chipped a tooth on a rock in the rice and dahl. Sure enough, as I ate overlooking the Ganga, it happened again. Another tooth! If this kept up, my free meals would turn out to be very expensive indeed. Instead of rice and watery dahl, for the price of repairing my teeth, I could have had vegetarian feasts catered right to my cave from Uttarkashi.

It started to rain. I made my way down to the river's edge and undressed and dunked. It was absolute ice water

---

[*]   The movie was *Mountains of the Moon,* directed by Bob Rafelson.

and froze me to my bones. I dressed frantically and then pulled the previous day's clothes from my shoulder bag to do laundry. By the time I was done washing my clothes, my hands were wrinkled and blue from the icy waters. I headed back to my cave in the cold downpour, without a raincoat. For all this, I was missing my daughter's sixteenth birthday. *Maybe, after all, it is time for me to leave.*

In my cave, I put on dry clothes, wrapped in my shawl and blankets, put on my wool hat and gloves, and started to meditate. Almost instantly I felt steeped in silent, pure, transcendent Being, a solid fullness of pure energy and consciousness evenly pervading everything, both within me and without. My mind dwelt in a realm beyond all complaints, beyond all thoughts even.

In that state, no amount of cold, rain, brain-burrowing beetles, or broken teeth could tempt me from my sole aim of knowing the Self. Here, in this freezing, damp cave, away from all attachments and other responsibilities, was my best chance to focus purely on the Self. It was the best chance I might have for a long time, maybe ever. I was not about to leave until I had given it all I had.

This determination, rooted in my very being, seemed to mark a significant leap in my detachment from everything and anything but the Self. As I continued to meditate, I felt an inner strength and resolve breaking a shell of familiar weakness that had previously bound me. The image of a baby bird breaking free of its shell came to mind.

I am bound by my likes and dislikes, an invisible web of attachment. Each attachment or aversion weakens me, saps my strength and integrity, and pushes my ideals further from being lived. I cherish comforts, relationships, tasty food, home, favorite places and things to do. All these are indeed gifts, but attachment to them diminishes me. It becomes a veil hiding the dignity of my true Self.

Then something Christ had said also came to mind:

If anyone comes to me and does not hate his father and mother, wife and children, brothers and sisters, even his own life, he cannot be a disciple of mine.*

That was strong language; Christ wasn't one to mince words. Clearly, however, he was not asking us to hate anyone, but rather to utterly reject our psychological attachments, to break free of everything that restricts, distracts, or dilutes our one-pointed passion for the Highest.

Break my attachments to my family? For a moment this thought made me wince: I did not want to forsake *everything* in my life . . .

Breaking attachment to my family does not make me less of a husband, less of a father. On the contrary, then I can give my family more love—real love, not attachment posing as love. The only way to fulfill my role of husband and father is to Be, freed, and allow love to flow in my actions.

Several hours later, after finishing meditation, I exited the cave. The night air was filled with a wonderful, hallowed silence. The moon illumined the mountains and forest in soft, celestial light, and the air shimmered with the magical presence of the Divine. I stood on the earth

---

*   Luke, 14:26

yet was in heaven. For a few minutes, standing all alone in that forest, I gazed at the mountains in the moonlight, drinking their beauty.

The Himalaya have stood firm throughout the eons—free of needs and attachments, radiating the silence of pure Being. This is how I, too, should live.

I recalled a phrase from St. John of the Cross: "Stand naked before God." Yes, that was it; we must stand naked. We must shed the clothing of ego, and so disappear into oneness with all.

In that moment, under the Himalayan night sky teeming with brilliant blue-white stars, it seemed I had disappeared. There was no me standing in the moonlight, only awareness—one with those mountains, the forest, moon, and the endless starry night sky. Everything I had experienced that day—from head cold, to fear of brain-burrowing beetles, to chipped tooth, to rainy bath—had played a role in my disappearance. Those events had each stirred familiar fears and attachments. In transcending those, I had transcended my small, familiar self.

But leaving what? Who am I now?

Only this simple awareness, an essence beyond individuality—transcendent, pure Being. This natural state of Being, beyond ego, felt so utterly simple—so simple, it held not a trace of individuality. It was universal.

What is Being?
The vast, ineffable Void.
It is love
Concentrated to infinity,
It is God
Everything
Nothingness.

It is I,
Without a trace of I-ness.

Let That, pure,
Shine in your heart
And know beyond knowing,
You simply are
Presence
Love, light, Truth
All.

The next day, I went to take my meal at the anna-kshetra. As usual, the young, lanky Tibetan server dished me a generous portion of rice and mung dahl with an equally generous warm smile. Nearly every day I was struck by how much happiness shone in his young face, which no doubt had seen its share of hardships. He was one of those remarkable people who radiated a beautiful spirituality, even without years of prolonged spiritual practice.

I had met many such people in India. Like this young man, typically they were simple and innocent, boasting no great achievements in the world. I speculated that their radiance was the blessing of having been raised in a spiritual family, or perhaps the result of having done a great deal of spiritual practice in a previous life. Yet that was only speculation. In truth, I had no idea. All I knew was they seemed blessed.

I sat on a broken-down rock wall, and began scooping up the simple but tasty meal. I chewed gingerly to sort out any rocks before they did further damage to my teeth. As I ate, I saw the Western sadhu who had joined me for lunch a few days before. He was passing by on the trail to the bridge, which led to the forest and my cave. I hoped he wouldn't spot me, but he did.

"Hello!" he yelled, and walked over to join me.

Mentally, I winced. I did not relish another strange conversation that would serve to interrupt and delay my daily routine. Yet I was also aware that with that very thought, my attachment was once more getting in the way of my openness to grace and an opportunity to give to another human being. I was a slow learner indeed!

I did my best to internally correct my attitude. *How could I be any less open and warm than the Tibetan server was towards me?*

As he approached, I noticed that he limped slightly, and as he got closer, I saw that he had bandages on his legs, arms, and forehead. On his foot was a nasty, bloody, open gash.

I pointed to his bandages with a questioning look.

"Oh these," he said with a wave of his hand, as if his wounds were insignificant. "I was climbing."

He sat next to me, took a deep breath as if walking had exhausted him, and was silent for a moment. Then gesturing towards the peak that towered above the Gangotri temple, he continued. "You see that mountain? It looks like you can just walk up there and sit in one of those pretty meadows, but it's not like that. No. You get up there, and you can't go anywhere. I mean you can't even come back down.

"I climbed up there yesterday and got caught where I couldn't move. I was stuck hanging on a damned cliff— couldn't go up, couldn't go down. Then I slipped and fell.

I was falling in mid-air off that mountain and thought I was done for. I thought, 'This is it!' and I just yelled out, '*Bhagavan!*'* I had just read that name in a book, so I yelled, 'Bhagavan!' and landed on a ledge. Saved my life that ledge did. But I got these nasty scratches. They'll heal soon enough though."

With a grimace, he massaged his right thigh. "Say, I'm going climbing this afternoon. Want to join me?"

I declined with a shake of my head. So that he would not take my refusal personally, I formed my fingers in chinmudra† and closed my eyes as if in meditation, to let him know that I would be occupied with my spiritual practices.

"Ah, you're established in your sadhana here. That's what I want to do, but I'm having a hell of a time finding a cave that will do me through the winter. These bastards that run the ashrams won't do anything for you. All they care about is the ruuupeee." He uttered the word "rupee" with disdain. "They're all corrupt. The only honest ones here are the businessmen. At least with them you know it's the money they're after.

"But I'll beat them, I will. You'll see. I'm staying. They say no Westerner can stay the winter here, only Indian nationals. We'll see about that. I know the Indian army. I know how to beat them. I can climb. I can go where they can't follow me." His face was flushed with anger, and he talked loud and fast.

"It's not just the people running the ashrams," he continued. "The sadhus are just as bad. They don't like white

---

*   The supreme Lord.

†   Joining the tips of the forefinger and thumb, with the remaining fingers held straight.

skin. They think they're superior. They won't accept me as one of them." He shook his head slowly. "No, never."

Having finished my meal, I saluted him with joined palms and a sympathetic smile, then mimed that I had to go to the Ganga and bathe and do my laundry.

I felt for him. Indeed, I found myself liking him a great deal; he was so earnest. But he sabotaged himself by his conviction the world was against him. He was constantly in a mode of defense and attack. If he could only walk a bit more lightly, radiate a little more positivity and openness, how differently the world might respond to him.

After bathing, I walked along the market street lined with sadhus. Their faces were aglow as they greeted me with warm smiles, calls of "Hari Om!" or "Mauna Baba!" and joined palms—as if they were cheering me on in my sadhana. I recalled the Italian and his impression of the sadhus. No doubt he was not imagining things. I didn't doubt the sadhus were wary of him, for he must appear to them rather strange.

The feeling you put out is the feeling you get back. If you put out tension, you receive tension in return. If you put out love, sooner or later, you will get love back. "As you sow, so shall you reap," is not a trite statement, but the secret of living in grace.

This is also how you create your reality. You see the world through the lens of your mind and heart. In that sense, you can only know what you are, and the world becomes (for you) exactly what you know.

Then again, I had known sincere people who tried to live this principle by doing good deeds, which should lead to a positive, happy life, yet their lives remained tense and unhappy. How could this be?

The key to living in grace is not the occasional good deed, but the feeling with which you do everything. With each act, each thought, you radiate feeling into the universe, and life responds in kind. In other words, to live in grace, you must radiate grace.

That thought fascinated me. Most people seemed to think that God in heaven is the source of grace in our lives, but the source of grace is actually within you, though beyond your ego. Grace comes to you as you radiate it.

How can you radiate grace? According to the Philosophy of Yoga, you don't have to do anything to radiate grace. Divine consciousness is your essential nature; you just have to get out of the way. Just remove (or greatly reduce) the veil of the ego to become transparent to the inner source of grace and love, your innermost Self. Then you radiate grace through every word and action, even by simply being. Compassion, love, gratitude, humility, joy, are your very nature. I had felt this around Maharishi, Amma, and Dinesha. They radiated these qualities as the sun radiates light. If they could do it, why couldn't anyone?

Yet I knew from experience this is not so easy. I had meditated for decades and could lay no claim to such a state. Life will repeatedly test your ability to dance in the midst of trials without reacting, to dance with love and joy despite anything and everything. You will encounter criticism, the negativity of others, disappointments, sickness, pain. Sooner or later, these and other problems are sure to find even the most blessed person. But such tests and trials—and inevitable failings—at least keep you humble and real. They are the way by which you must travel if you are to integrate what you gain in prayer and meditation.

To master this dance of life, you must master yourself.

But can mastery of this dance of life ever be gained, really? I could not say. Perhaps a degree of mastery can be gained upon the dissolution of the ego, upon enlightenment. Yet to speak of mastery . . . that seemed too bold.

I remembered something my first teacher, Maharishi Mahesh Yogi, had said from time to time. He admonished his teachers not to speak of perfection. He said that as long as you have a human body, perfection was impossible, in any state of consciousness. He went on to say that enlightenment should not be thought of as something supernormal; rather, it was just normal human life.

I liked that. It was what I had seen for myself when I was 18 and thrown into the Infinite.* Normal does not mean ordinary or the societally accepted norm; rather, it means having cleansed all the subconscious twists and turns; it means purifying mind, body, and energetic body, so these function in harmony and balance, free of distortion. In that state of simple normalcy, your Essence, which is unbounded light, intelligence, joy, and love shines effortlessly. That is normal human life. That is a life of grace. Not a life of perfection.

This reminded me of another Indian saint I admired, Sri Nisargadatta Maharaj, who used to say the same. He always equated enlightenment with normalcy and confounded questions begging a more sensational view. For instance, when asked about whether he could perform miracles, he replied:

The world itself is a miracle. I am beyond miracles—I am absolutely normal.

---

*   See Introduction.

CHAPTER 8

Divine Science

What is true Knowledge?
Knowing I am all,
Not a particle of creation
Separate from myself.
All else by the name "knowledge"
Is ignorance.

The next morning's meditation began with an experience of indescribable peace. In fact, a phrase came to me: "the Self of Peace." I was That, pure Being, pure Silence. But as I continued to sit, that peace began to warm up into something else: energy, pure energy. Every cell of me was stretched beyond its capacity by that brilliant energy and wholeness. My head felt like a super light bulb with 10,000 watts coursing through it. Every nerve in my body was being stretched by an immense power. That power had nothing to do with my individuality. It was pure, transcendent spiritual energy.

And then the pain came. It began as slight body aches and inner heat, growing more and more intense, until my whole body burned as if I were being sacrificed on a divine pyre.

The words of St. John of the Cross came to me. Speaking of the necessary purification of the soul on the spiritual path, in *The Dark Night* he writes:

All is meted out according to God's will and the greater or lesser amount of imperfection that must be purged from each one. In the measure of the degree of love to which God wishes to raise a soul, he humbles it with greater or less intensity, or for a longer or shorter period of time. [*]

I could only trust this was the reason for that inner burning, that I had not contracted some flu bug, or worse. I could only trust that, as St. John of the Cross and others had said, such purification was necessary for union with the clear Light of the Divine in this lifetime. Apparently, I had quite a measure of imperfection to be purged.

After about an hour-and-a-half of burning and aching, I simply had to stop meditating. I decided to take a break to do some yogasanas outside.

I set out my yoga mat on the boulder outside my cave. The sun was behind the clouds, but at least it wasn't raining. Within minutes of beginning asanas, the inner pain of purification began to dissolve. A few more minutes, and not only did it dissolve, but it was transformed.

---

[*]   St. John of the Cross. *The Collected Works of St. John of the Cross.* Trans. Kieran Kavanaugh and Otilio Rodriguez. Washington, D.C.: Washington Province of Discalced Carmelites, ICS Publications, 1973: 329.

Again, I felt peace and well-being. In fact, it was amazing: from agony and angst to peace, evenness, and a sense of emotional balance in a few minutes of yoga.

Over the years of practice, I had often experienced asanas to be a wonderful gift. Not only do they help to break up crystallized patterns in the body and mind, but when performed with care and attention, they soothe, homogenize, and balance the energies and emotions. They can also be grounding when meditation taps into powerful spiritual energy such as I had experienced that morning.

That is one reason I loved India's spiritual science, represented by the traditions of Yoga and Tantra: It's not random mysticism; it's really a scientific approach to experience the Essence of life. It is a science in that it systematically lays out an array of practices that have pre-dictable and reproducible effects. Seekers for thousands of years have validated these effects in their lives. These practices are wonderful in that they not only accelerate your growth towards your spiritual goal, but help you stay balanced and healthy as you progress.

I sometimes wondered what St. John of the Cross would have thought of yogasanas and the other techniques pre-scribed by this science. It sounds glib to suggest it, but I wonder if his dark night of the soul might not have been quite so dark had he had such a technology available to him. At least I can say from my own personal experience that without the balancing effect of the various techniques,[*] as well as Ayurveda (the traditional Indian medical system that is a sister science of Yoga), my road would certainly have been a lot rockier.

That said, I have nothing but the greatest admiration for St. John of the Cross, St. Teresa of Avila, and the many

---

[*]   See ajayan.com for more information.

other Christian mystics and mystics of other spiritual traditions. Such great souls were propelled forward primarily by force of their pure love for the Divine, and they achieved heights that I can barely imagine. Yet for the rest of us, I believe a systematic approach is a great blessing.

After finishing asanas, I returned to my cave to start pranayama. Gradually, my breathing became fine and prolonged. At one point it transformed: I was breathing not merely air, but pure energy. Literally, I was breathing in energy! This energy felt cooling, vacuous, space-like; with each breath, I was being filled with ecstatic space.

As I continued, my mind became laser focused, my attention indescribably fine and intense. Then it was as if an inner door opened, and I was forcibly pulled through it. No longer was I in my body; rather, I was an observer in the vastness of outer space, surrounded by galaxies of stars. This felt as real as sitting on the boulder outside my cave had felt a minute earlier—I was floating in outer space—only I was aware that it was also the space of inner awareness. Inner and outer space were one and the same.

After what seemed like a few minutes, the scene faded and I was again in my body. I had stopped pranayama, probably when I had been pulled into that state. I lay down to come out of the experience smoothly, my body feeling like it was made of blissful space.

The whole experience was mind boggling, yet it also made sense to me in that spiritual practices are intended to refine perception. That is, they attune the mind and senses to perceive the subtler levels of existence on the way to perceiving the Divine. As modern Physics has shown, matter actually *is* energy. So when this remarkable gift—the human nervous system and mind—directly experiences the subtle layers of existence, perceives matter as energy, why should that be surprising?

But what of that shift into a cosmic state where inner and outer space were one? Perhaps it had something to do with another conclusion revealed by quantum physics: infinite correlation, everything is everywhere, everything is contained within every particle of existence. This means the entire universe is within us; inner and outer space *are* one. Many mystics have expressed this. In his poem "Auguries of Innocence," William Blake wrote:

To see a World in a Grain of Sand
And a Heaven in a Wild Flower,
Hold Infinity in the palm of your hand
And Eternity in an hour.

If this is the truth, and we have the potential, why not live this? Most of us barely scratch the surface of this gift of human life. We live only a fraction of life, like insects that see only one slim range of light, or hear one extreme range of sound. Yet we have the potential for so much more . . .

As I approached the annakshetra, I saw my Western sadhu friend was seated cross-legged on the ground, eating.

"Hari Om!" he called to me.

I got my food and sat down next to him.

"Well, my things were stolen out of my room yesterday," he began abruptly, shaking his head slowly in disgust. "Yep. Well, not *all* my things. I have this shawl, you see, so I won't freeze. And they didn't take my cooking pot. But they got my blanket and pack, the bastards. You can't trust Indians. They'll steal anything."

I had to admit I had seen a disconcerting amount of petty theft in India.

"You have to lock your room, and I didn't. I should have known better. At my kutir (hut) in Rajasthan, I could leave the door open and no one would steal a thing. I made friends with the army there, you see. I made tea for them, so they wouldn't steal from me. But they didn't respect my sadhana. I'd be meditating, and they'd want me to make them tea. So I built another kutir away in the hills."

I scribbled on a notepad, "Where are you from?" I had thought his accent was Italian, but I wasn't sure.

He read it with a glance. "Where I'm from doesn't matter, friend. It's where I'm going that counts. But I'll tell you if you like." He took a deep breath and began. "I was born in northern Italy, but my father moved to Australia when I was a teenager, so I lived there for a few years. Since then I've been all over Asia.

"I started a business in Hong Kong—went well for a while. The police caught on to it, though, and kicked us out." His blue eyes flashed bright as he studied me for a reaction.

I nodded.

"Then I came to India," he continued, "About ten years ago, met a teacher in Rishikesh. He was my guru," he said shaking his head slowly, "but he didn't like me much. He gave me a hell of a time. One day, he told me to go, so I did. Since then I've been on my own. I told you I *got* the *Atman*, didn't I? Well, that was the real beginning for me.

"After that I started doing tapas. I didn't have any money at first, so I did the begging trip. Did pretty well at it, too," he added, sitting up straighter, "but that wasn't for me, so I moved to Rajasthan. Did tapas there for about six months; then someone found me and carried me to a hospital. I hadn't been paying much attention to eating and was just skin and bones. They found me on the floor in a heap, unconscious."

This amazed me. I couldn't imagine neglecting myself to such an extent. "Really?" I silently mouthed.

"Yep. After that some people began to offer me money. They thought maybe I was a saint." At this he sat up even straighter, flared his nostrils, and inhaled deeply.

"Yeah," he continued, "they offered me lots of money— *ridiculous* amounts of money. I turned them down, though. Just took what I needed, and I didn't need much. One businessman offered me enough money that I could have lived like a king for the rest of my life. I wouldn't take it, though.

"Anyway, now I'm here, and this is where I'm staying. But I haven't found a place for my sadhana yet. They're all playing monopoly—the ashrams, the government, the army—manipulating for the big rupees. They don't want to help."

By this time, we had finished eating. I had an impulse to tell him about my cave. It was the best one I knew of that wasn't owned by an ashram, and when I left Gangotri, it could be just the thing for him. Then again, I dreaded the thought of him knowing my whereabouts; he might start visiting me, no doubt during my meditation hours. Still, I hated to see him so frustrated.

I took out my notebook and wrote: "Maybe sometime you should see my cave. It might work out for you when I leave."

He shook his head. "I don't want a cave. They're freezers, man. Now I'm thinking of a kutir; the sun warms a kutir real nice."

Relieved, I wobbled my head and got up to go.

He got up too. "Do you want to go climbing this afternoon?" he asked.

I shook my head no and put my hands in chinmudra, indicating that I would be meditating.

"That's all right. Another fellow's coming with me, but he's a real bastard. He thinks he's enliiiightened," he said, his eyes flashing sarcasm. "He's pulling all kinds of power trips on me, trying to control me and make me his devotee. I've abused power before. It comes back at you, fast. I've had so much power, my third eye was popping out of my forehead, but that's not where it's at. You'll suffer if you abuse power. Take my advice, don't ever do it, friend. Keep humble, simple; that's what I try to do."

I was growing fonder of this fellow. He seemed fairly crazy, but he certainly had a few things right.

That afternoon, back at the cave, meditation was simply sitting in an ocean of pristine, blissful Being. That state is God. No one could ever convince you otherwise. When you sit in God, you know it—an endless ocean of divinity, light, and absolute peace. Undoubtedly this depth of experience was the fruit of the recent days of burning in meditation and that morning's cosmic experience.

I know that many think such experiences are impossible today, reserved for seekers of the distant past or for a few lucky ones in the present, but as every teacher I've ever heard of declares: divine love, bliss, knowledge, are the birthright of us all. As a matter of fact, the Infinite is your own essential nature—how can it be available only to someone else?

To realize your divine Essence, you need only take the prescribed steps. The science of Yoga and the Tantric paths are systematic, but all the great spiritual traditions of the world must lead to the same Truth. You need only follow the path that suits you best, with full faith and commitment. If it becomes the all-consuming priority in your life, then you cannot but progress rapidly towards your goal.

Time and again, this had been made clear to me. Intensity and single-minded devotion create an irresistible force, like the Ganga, cutting through the mountains of ignorance and conditioning that separate us from knowing the Infinite. Those who walk their spiritual path with sincere, one-pointed dedication will not be disappointed.

After a few hours of meditation, which passed like a few minutes, a faint thought arose:

My own consciousness is none other than the eternal Self.

As I savored that truth, the memory of a friend I had not seen or even thought of in many years came to mind. Once a student of meditation, he had converted to fundamentalist Christianity and had renounced meditation and anything to do with the East. A few weeks after his conversion, he asked me, "I don't understand why Indian Philosophy places such an emphasis on consciousness. Consciousness is just a relative phenomenon, created by the functioning of the brain. There's nothing divine about it."

As I recalled this conversation, a Sanskrit phrase came to me as if in answer to his question: *"prajnanam Brahma"* (consciousness is Brahman).

Instantly, this phrase seemed to plunge my mind again into pure Being, this time so deeply that I disappeared. After some time, I reappeared, filled with awe. What was that seemingly all-powerful phrase that had dissolved my mind with a single thought? How could it do that? What was the significance of *prajnanam Brahma*?

I knew this phrase was one of the four, classic *mahavakyas* (great aphorisms), from some of India's most famous scriptures relating to the philosophy of non-duality, the *Upanishads*. The mahavakyas are considered the most concentrated expressions of Truth, traditionally spoken by the guru to the disciple to confirm and integrate the disciple's dawning realization of Brahman, the all-encompassing, universal Self. Yet I had always taken the meaning of prajnanam Brahma on an obvious level, without bothering to contemplate it deeply.

Again, I thought it, *prajnanam Brahma,* and again my mind dissolved into the Infinite. This time as I emerged from that blissful, deep silence, the meaning of that phrase as it related to my friend's question suddenly seemed clear. In fact, it struck me as an insight so basic to human existence, so holistic and filled with a sense of Truth, that it seemed a secret of the universe. Essentially it was this:

Consciousness is necessary to know anything. You are conscious of the world, of yourself, of others, of your thoughts and feelings; nothing whatsoever can be known except through consciousness. Further, consciousness expands to encompass whatever is known. You can be conscious of the earth, the sun, the galaxy, the entire universe, of God; there is no limit to the capacity of consciousness to know. There is nothing too great for consciousness. It expands to encompass whatever we focus on. It is therefore greater than whatever we know. It is the Ultimate, and it is within each of us.

*Yet consciousness is invisible. You do not know conscious-
ness. Why?*

*Consciousness is not an object to be known. It is pure
subject. It is the irreducible essence of the knower—of all
knowers, from the lowest to the highest. Even God must
know by virtue of consciousness—for what else knows
but consciousness? Consciousness is the innermost subject, the Self, of all beings—and is God's innermost Self,
too. Thus God dwells within all beings, and that divine
consciousness is Brahman— "prajnanam Brahma."*

But the next minute, another question arose: What
is the relationship between pure consciousness and pure
Being?

*Consciousness is not separate from Being. Consciousness,
dwelling in Itself, knowing Itself, is the ground state of
Being, pure Existence. Since consciousness is Being, everything that Is is consciousness. Everything, from God to
even inanimate objects—rocks, mountains, fire, rivers, the
sky—is consciousness. That one all-pervasive wholeness
of consciousness is Brahman— "prajnanam Brahma."*

At this, I recalled something Amma had once said:
"When we enter into the higher states (planes) of sadhana
we can hear all these stones and wooden pieces talking to
us. They are not inert but conscious. Then it will become
clear that they are also talking. What is known as matter is
only at the empirical level. In reality, it is not there. Everything is one and the same consciousness."

The idea that even a rock is consciousness would
seem absurd to some. Yet modern physics reveals that all
matter is energy. Just a hundred years ago, what physicist
would have believed such an idea? The world does not

look like energy; it looks solid. What energy? Nonetheless, it is energy—and who is to say that all energy is not fundamentally consciousness?

Even prominent physicists recognize the central role consciousness plays in the universe. Max Planck, Nobel Laureate and the originator of quantum theory, said:

I regard consciousness as fundamental. I regard matter as derivative from consciousness. We cannot get behind consciousness. Everything that we talk about, everything that we regard as existing, postulates consciousness. *

For millennia, India's seers have held that Self-knowledge is the ultimate hidden treasure of all knowledge, that investigating the knower, consciousness, is the real frontier of physics, of all science, and of all philosophy and religion. Indeed, how can we know anything for certain, until we at least know the knower? The imperative of Socrates, "Know thyself," still stands.

I experienced these realizations not as philosophical arguments; rather, they bubbled up within me. On paper, they may seem dry or intellectual, yet that afternoon they were for me exciting and profound. A Tibetan Buddhist manuscript describes this experience.

One momentary glimpse of Divine Wisdom, born of meditation, is more precious than any amount of knowledge derived from merely listening to and thinking about religious teachings. †

---

* As quoted in *The Observer,* 25 January 1931.

† "The Supreme Path, the Rosary of Precious Gems," *Tibetan Yoga and Secret Doctrines*, Ed. W.Y. Evans Wentz, 2nd edition, Oxford University Press, XXIV. 4: 90.

CHAPTER 9

Significance and Insignificance

Deluded, we take on myriad identities:
Father, mother, sister, brother,
"I am writer, attorney, plumber,"
But dig deeper and find
That all is nothing,
Hallowed hollowness.

So let this be my meditation:
I am not this body,
No one's father, no one's son,
Not these thoughts, this mind,
Nor the intellect making these statements.
I am not anything.
In fact, there is no "I."
Now rest in That which remains,
Presence—pure, silent, undefined—
The Source of all "I am's."

Finally, there was a break in the rain. Snow-capped mountains reappeared where clouds had been, pine needles glittered in the sun, and a gentle, summery breeze carried the fragrance of fresh, moist forest. Even Ganga's roar sounded happier. As a lover awakens beauty in the beloved, the sun's embrace awakened the forest's charm. It was definitely time to get out of my cave and take a long walk.

I remembered the cave on the other side of the Rudra Ganga that Krishnadas had pointed out to me weeks before. Perhaps on some future trip to Gangotri I would want to live there—but I should see it first. I began walking along the way Krishnadas had pointed out, to explore the Rudra Ganga.

I trudged sharply up the mountain above the Rudra Ganga canyon. All the while the river dropped further and further below, until it appeared to be a small, distant stream. Finally, I came to a fork in the trail. One branch of the trail continued up; the other, an unnervingly narrow one, headed down towards the river.

Only a few inches wide, this little-used descending trail was treacherous to say the least. Carved out of loose dirt and shifting gravel, it overhung a merciless abyss of hundreds of feet, and always the trail's surface was slanted towards the sheer drop. Krishnadas's idea of a trail was death with a bow tied around it.

I cautiously began the descent. For thirty minutes, I warily shuffled down the treacherous trail. Finally, with great relief, I reached the canyon floor.

Surrounding me now was an entirely new world— lush, verdant, vibrant with purple, red, and yellow wildflowers—a perfect, untouched garden. A series of magnificent waterfalls cascaded from a towering chasm above. A faint breeze carried their refreshing cool mist mixed with the sweet fragrance of flowers. For a few minutes, I sat on a boulder, savoring this scene; then I headed downstream, strolling along a gentle path through flowering bushes.

Soon I reached a point where two thin logs had been placed to form a bridge over the raging Rudra Ganga. It was the only way to the cave on the other side. Again, I debated about turning back. Here the river crashed around boulders in a wild, explosive dance; if I slipped off those logs, no one would ever find the pieces. Having come that far, though, I could not see turning back. I straddled the wet, slick logs, and carefully shimmied across, my feet dangling a few inches above the raging rapids.

I had guessed that one slip into the river might well have meant death, but just how true this was hit me only after I had crossed the logs and walked 20 yards further downstream. Here, just out of view of the log bridge, the river gushed over a precipice, dropped twenty feet, and shattered onto a jagged boulder, sending a glittering spray in all directions. A human body caught in that waterfall would not fare well. Doubtless the Rudra Ganga, though, would rush on without notice.

In the face of that rugged and powerful nature, I could not but feel my smallness as a mere man. How short and delicate was a human life compared to that river and canyon that had formed over millennia and would flow for centuries more.

Only in the protected and buffered world of man—in the cities, villages, and wherever else we have molded the earth to fill our needs—can we maintain the illusion that we have mastered nature, are masters of life. There man may be king—but not on a treacherous ledge in the mountains, or shimmying across a torrent on a piece of tree. Here, the buffers are gone, and you feel the vastness and power of this universe, and know that you are dust. Life is a precious gift. We are blessed just to be alive. We aren't masters at all.

I soon reached the "cave," but as it turned out, it was only a dark hole in a cliff wall just big enough to lie down in. I would have liked to see the Englishman that could live in that indentation for six days, much less six months.

Even though the cave was a dud, as I made my way back up the trail towards the safety of my own wonderful cave, I felt grateful for the afternoon's adventure and the perspective it had given me. It seemed healthy to be reminded of my insignificance.

Feeling our insignificance humbles and opens our hearts to life's vastness and mystery. Only then might we find the vastness within ourselves.

It reminded me of something Amma was fond of saying: "To be a hero, you must first become a zero."

That evening, as I meditated, my mind again swam in an inner world of light-illumined Truth. A short phrase from the Ninth Mandala of the *Rig Veda* came to mind that fit the experience perfectly, *"the world in which the sun is placed,"** a celestial realm filled with the golden-white light of God. That world was the heaven within, an inner universe, which spoke of our significance.

Again, as a few days before, sublime insights filled my meditation. Sitting in my cave in that peaceful corner of Himalayan forest, the night sky glittering with stars of blue-white brilliance overhead, the Himalayas whispered their eternal songs of Being. Those whispers were not my

---

* Rig Veda, IX. 7. 10: 7

own, of that I was sure. They were a gift of the purity of the Himalaya and of all the saints and sages who had meditated there. I was only fortunate enough to be there, listening.

To feel the silence of Being is sublime,
Brings peace and poetry to the soul,
But knowing you are eternal Silence
Is life's true Goal.

About six months before coming to the Himalayas, a most powerful process of meditation had been revealed to me. It was far beyond any other technique I knew of, for it consistently took my mind beyond spiritual experience to rest in transcendent Being. At the same time, it primed my mind to have much subtler and clearer experiences during the other portions of my practices. I had been given this technique in my meditation spontaneously—by grace it had seemed to me, or perhaps by the guidance of an enlightened sage no longer in his body.*

---

*   I later learned that this practice, in all its detail, was taught by Shankara, the great Advaitic master of the late 8th and early 9th century. My first teacher's teacher, Swami Brahmananda Saraswati, with whom I have long felt a deep connection, was an eminent Shankaracharya of Jyotir Math. It seemed to me that perhaps it was he guiding me. Be that as it may, this instruction was a gift.

Midway through that most powerful portion of my practice, the thought of Amma came. She was somewhere in the U.S.A., on her world tour, and my heart suddenly longed to be with her. The next moment, Amma was no longer on the opposite side of the world. She was not anywhere else at all. She was inside me. Not only was she inside me, she *was* me.

> *Before Self-realization, you may pray to your idea of a Higher Power or to a saint to feel their presence and receive their grace. If you are fortunate, you may at times experience a deep connection with that divine being. Yet ultimately, Higher Power, saint, or guru is nowhere else at all, nor is He/She a separate being or person. In truth, you pray to your own inner Essence. All is none other than your Self.*

After finishing meditation, I crouched through the cave door and went outside. As I stood up, the mountains opposite me caught my eye. Cutting through a layer of clouds, those massive cliffs, stolid observers throughout the millennia, seemed so silent. The stillness of Being emanated from them almost visibly—a subtle, shimmering light. That shimmering stillness hung in the forest's air, and just to breathe it gave peace.

I had been silent for one month, and the stillness that exuded from those mountains I felt within as well. What joy lies in that soothing balm of holy silence, that peace, which is also indescribable power. If only everyone could experience it, who would not want to meditate?

That inner silence is the wonder; merely refraining from speech is only an aid to experience it. Still, the discipline of observing silence by not speaking does deepen your inner experience. I had first discovered that power by accident, on a retreat in 1972-73 on the southern coast of Spain with Maharishi Mahesh Yogi.

Perhaps a thousand or more of us were being trained to teach the Transcendental Meditation Program®. As part of the course, we observed silence for the first ten days of January, 1973, meditating almost around the clock. On the tenth day, I stood in a line outside a dining hall, waiting for dinner to be served. A friend walked by me. That day we were scheduled to break silence, so I softly whispered his first name, just loud enough for him to hear me.

With that whisper, a rush of energy rose in my body. The next thing I knew I was laying on the ground looking up into my friend's face. With the exertion of that whisper, I had fainted. Such is the energy involved in speech, though normally we are not aware of it.

Conserving that energy through observing a vow of silence allows thinking to become effortlessly clear, and an inner calm develops that feels like divine sunlight filling the mind. In fact, after some time in silence, you can feel a light and blissful energy gathering throughout the body, especially in the head.

Besides conserving spiritual energy, silence also shows a different way to be. If you are in silence, when someone is rude or thoughtless, you cannot incriminate yourself by voicing your reaction. Rather, by your silence you simulate patience. When you feel angry or negative, you can't speak it out—and later you are inevitably glad for it. Silence thereby reveals your shortcomings to yourself alone, and helps uplift you to your higher Self. Silence is a dear friend guiding you towards your freedom. As the 13th Century Tibetan Lama, Sqaskya Pandita, wrote:

> Silence is the means of avoiding misfortune:
> The talkative parrot is shut up in a cage;
> Other birds, which cannot talk, fly about freely.

As I stood imbibing the silence of those sacred peaks, the words of Lao Tsu came to me, *"He who knows does not speak; he who speaks does not know."*

In that moment, the meaning of that verse seemed clearer to me than ever before: One who is yet a separate, finite experiencer may *speak* of the Infinite. He may know *about* the Infinite from reading and even from transient personal experience, but he has not yet realized he *is* That. Whereas one who has disappeared into the Infinite is silence itself, indescribable, beyond words. He knows, but does not speak, for he knows he cannot be spoken of.

Rarely is it graceful to talk about oneself. The supreme Self, the source of everything, is eternal silence—and so, eternally graceful.

But then what of the many sages who have taught and guided others to the Self? What of those who have written the scriptures? For that matter, what of Lao Tsu himself?

The enlightened ones may or may not speak, but either way, their inmost Self remains eternally silent. Do they speak, or do they remain silent? Always, only silent.

CHAPTER 10

Invasion

Simply Be.
If you can,
You will see
There is no me
Messing up the works.
Just the universe
Doing exactly what it wants to
Through you.

The next day the Italian fellow was again eating lunch at the ashram when I arrived. Just as I finished silently giving thanks for my meal and opened my eyes, he spit out a rock.

"Damn rocks! Don't know why I eat here," he said, shaking his head in disgust. "You know, there's another annakshetra over there," he waved his hand in the direction of the other side of the Ganga and downstream, "and they serve a reeeal meal. Not watery dahl and rice with rocks, but chapattis, thick dahl, curried vegetables, and rice pudding. You can even get milk there, man!"

This caught my interest. I wrote a question on my notepad, "Will they let me in?" By no means could I assume they would, for I was neither a wandering Indian holy man nor a beggar, and my white skin equated with wealth in the minds of many Indians. I had already been turned down by the annakshetra where my friend Krishnadas ate.

He slapped his thigh. "Of course! They *love* your type. You can go to the head of the line," he said with absolute confidence.

It sounded good, but still I felt uncomfortable with the idea. I already had an arrangement here, and I stepped on no one's toes. There, you never knew; they might take offense. I scribbled in my notepad, "I wouldn't feel comfortable. I'll just stay here."

"Look, it's easy," he said. "Just walk in and they serve you, no questions asked. Just pretend you know what you're doing. A sadhu *always* knows what he's doing. He never asks a question. That's their code." He paused and then asked sincerely, "Please come."

He was so earnest that I could hardly turn him down. "When do they serve?" I wrote in my pad.

He smiled happily. "5:00 sharp. But better get there at 4:30 to get a seat."

"In the afternoon?" I scribbled.

"Yeah."

I made a disappointed face and shook my head, then put my fingers in chinmudra to show that was in the middle of my meditation time. This was not just an excuse. As much as I would have liked to do this for him, the time it would take for the extra trip to town and to digest the meal, would mean cutting a minimum of 4 hours of meditation from my routine. I could not sacrifice my sadhana for rice pudding and thick dahl.

"Ah, I see," he said, his head literally hanging down with disappointment. "Well, I'm leaving in a few days."

I started in surprise.

"Yeah," he continued, "not for good. I need to get some things I have in Rajasthan. I'll be gone about a month. Then I'll be back to stay the winter."

"Have you found a kutir?" I wrote.

"No. Don't know what I'll do. No one will help. If I have to, I'll sleep on somebody's porch, and when they see me freezing in the snow, we'll see what they do. They won't let me die, I'm sure of that."

Well, that was one approach. It would probably work, too, but I felt that my cave was a better option for him. With the right supplies, in my cave he could survive the 20 degrees below zero and ten feet of snow, and do his sadhana all winter in peace and solitude. It could be ideal for him.

I could not help but feel the impulse to show it to him, and since he was leaving for a month, doing so would pose no peril to my privacy. Besides, I wanted to help him. He was in need, after all, and no one else was step-ping forward. Yet an uneasy feeling plagued me at the prospect of telling him the whereabouts of my cave. I was not sure why, but it seemed a mistake. Nonetheless, it was time for me to start being more selfless, and it might save him a great deal of disappointment and frustration. I fig-ured if there was any mistake in showing him the cave, it could only be a slight one.

"You should come and see my cave," I wrote, "I think it might work for you."

His face lit up. "I'd love to. When?"

I pointed to the ground, meaning "today," then held up one finger for "one o'clock."

"Today. One o'clock," he said, following my meaning perfectly. "Okay. We'll meet here?"

I nodded.

After bathing and washing my laundry in the Ganga, I returned to meet him, and we began the trek to my cave. On the way, he talked nonstop of the politicking and corruption rampant in the little Himalayan hamlet of Gangotri.

As we neared the cave, he was clearly struck by its ideal location, not to mention its sturdy, lockable door. Beaming, he ran the last thirty feet up to it. I caught up with him, unlocked the door, and showed him inside. I confess I felt no small pleasure in sharing the secret of my idyllic little Hobbit hovel. He was thrilled. He agreed that it was his best chance to survive the winter in Gangotri and began eagerly making a flurry of plans.

"Two 100-gallon tanks of water would do you for the winter," he said, his eyes lighting keenly. "You could melt snow for more, and with a kerosene stove, you wouldn't need so much wood. It should be possible, really. You'd have to dig yourself out of the cave when it snowed, of course. It would be damn cold, but I think I could survive it."

His ardor played on my own enthusiasm for my cave, and I wanted to show him how he could descend to the Ganga for water access, which would make living in the cave year around much more practical. I wrote him a note to that effect, and then began leading him down the goat trail towards the rock slide where I had nearly met my end. I figured that all he would need was a good rope, and he could climb down both the slide and the 30-foot drop to the beach. Since he was a skilled rock climber, I had little doubt that he would see its potential.

When we reached the top of the rock slide, however, he took one look and shook his head. "I wouldn't go down this. I don't think we could get back up." To emphasize his point, he kicked at some of the grass to which I had previously clung for dear life and sent it flying down to the beach below.

I shook my head and tried to mime that I had gone down and gotten back up, and that all he would need was a good rope, but he interrupted me.

"Come with me," he said. "I know an easier way. I went down there a couple of weeks ago when I was looking for a cave. There's a *huge* cave there. Somebody even filled it with firewood, but it's freezing cold because it's so close to the river."

An easier way? How could that be? But if he really did know of a path to the river, that was fantastic news. I could bathe and get my water right here instead of in town. It began to look like helping him had not been a mistake at all, but a blessing for me.

I followed a few steps behind him as he briskly strode along the top of the canyon for about a hundred yards. Then we began a treacherous descent down a nearly vertical slope studded with huge pines. I had previously tried that way, not because it had looked promising, but because Krishnadas had once pointed it out to me as the only way to the river. I had found it an impossible approach.

Nonetheless, I continued following him, trusting that perhaps he had found Krishnadas's actual route. As we descended, however, footholds and handholds became fewer and fewer, and I began wondering if I was going to survive the afternoon. One slip and we'd tumble down two hundred feet of cliff. This "easier way" was beginning to feel like a death trap.

A few more steps and I recalled the fall he had taken a couple of weeks ago. How could I let such a nut lead me? I stopped and turned to climb back up the cliff to safety.

Seeing that I was deserting him, he tried to reassure me in an apologetic tone, "Oh, sorry, this isn't the way, but don't worry," he pointed to a cliff twenty yards to our right, "I think it's over there."

Again, I followed him, but only a short way. This second trail was clearly another death trap. It simply was not worth the risk to me. I had learned my lesson. I was not in Gangotri, after all, to take stupid chances with my life. I could continue to bathe in town. Now I just wanted to get to my afternoon meditation.

Seeing me turn back for a second time, he said, "No, no. Don't worry. You won't fall. You won't fall, and if you do, I'll catch you."

Right. I wanted to remind him that *he* had fallen when he thought he wouldn't, but I could not do so without breaking my silence. I simply turned and began climbing the cliff without looking back. He followed me.

"Well, okay," he said once we had reached the top. "It was more difficult than I remembered."

We walked back to my cave in silence.

When we reached the cave, he looked at me sheepishly. "There are a few things I'd like to collect for the winter, but I don't have any place to store them. Would it be all right if I store them here with you? You can use them if you like."

I inwardly groaned at the prospect of him cluttering my cave with his things. I had no need for anything more than what I already had—two changes of clothes, some blankets, my hat, and a shawl. Nevertheless, feeling that I should help him, I wrote him a note saying that if he could store them out of the way, it would be fine.

"I'll go get them now," he said, dashing off before I could pick up my notepad to ask him to wait until tomorrow, when he would not interrupt my meditation. I consoled myself with the assurance that one afternoon's messed up schedule was a small price to pay to help him.

An hour later he returned carrying several five-gallon tins with their tops cut off. "These will make good water storage," he said, putting them on the ground with care. Then he pulled some rags and stainless steel plates out of one of the tins. "You can use these plates to eat on, and these rags for something. And over there," he added with enthusiasm, pointing to the trail to town, "is a bed and pots and pans. I carried them part of the way, but all of it was too heavy for me. Would you help?"

Again, I moaned to myself. A bed? In my cave? Suddenly life in Gangotri was becoming complicated. I wrote him a note asking him where he got all these things.

"Well, I got the tins from the deserted cave at the end of the trail, and the bed and pots from a deserted cave at the beginning of the trail."

I felt a sudden shot of anxiety. The cave at the end of the trail was Krishnadas's old cave, Pandu Guha. That meant that the tins, plates, and rags were his. The other cave, I knew, was an ashram's, and it wasn't deserted at all. Perhaps the Swami staying there had been out for his meal. These items weren't much by Western standards, but they meant a modicum of convenience and comfort for those Swamis. My impulsive friend had nothing less than stolen them. Now he wanted to store them in my cave!

I wrote him a note: "Those caves aren't deserted. I know who lives there."

"No," he replied, shaking his head solemnly. Continuing in a sincere tone, he said, "Believe me, it's not improper for us to take these things. If you don't lock your door, it's fair game. Trust me. That's how it is in India."

This was too much. I wanted to remind him how just a few days ago, he had been outraged when his things had been stolen. In any case, I wanted none of this. Up until this moment, I had enjoyed a good relationship with everyone in Gangotri. These Swamis were my friends, and I would not harbor their stolen belongings. Before I could pick up my pen and pad, though, he was on his feet.

"Come. At least look at the bed," he urged. "It's just your size, and if you don't want to sleep on it, it'll make good firewood." He turned and began climbing up the hill to the trail. Seeing me standing unmoved, he waved me on. I finally followed him, but with the intention of returning the bed to the cave from where he had stolen it; then I would return the tins and other goods.

As we crested the hill that hid my cave from the nature trail, three rough-looking men standing on the trail met us with stony stares. Their khaki-colored clothes identified them as members of the Indian army.

Oh, great! The authorities have already been alerted to the thefts.

The one who seemed to be in charge lifted his hand for us to stop. "You have camera?" the man asked us in stilted English.

My Italian friend and I looked at each other. As far as I knew, he had not stolen a camera. We both shook our heads no.

Now the leader of the small squad pointed to me. "*You* have camera," he said with certainty.

Again, I shook my head.

"You have camera!" he insisted.

Suddenly it hit me: They were not after us for the stolen goods. They just wanted us to take their picture.

I made a motion with my hands as if to say, "Ah, get out of here." His stubbornness seemed positively bizarre, and I had no camera. I just wanted to get to my meditation.

At my motion, his face flushed with anger. He took a few steps closer to us, and his companions followed. My only thought was: If only I had not shown my cave to this crazy Italian, these guys would never have seen me. I would not have all this junk lying outside my cave. I would not have nearly gotten killed on the cliff, and I'd be meditating peacefully.

Suddenly my companion stepped forward between the three men and me. Lifting his joined hands as if imploring them in mock prayer, he yelled, "Shanti! Shanti!" ("Peace! Peace!") His tone was aggressive, not prayerful. Then dramatically bowing at my feet, he touched my sneakers with theatrical reverence. "Guru! Guru!" he said pointing to me as he knelt before me. Again, he was on his feet, facing the three nonplussed men menacingly. "You violent men! Bad men! You kill!" he shouted. Then pointing to himself and me, he added with dramatic pride, "We sadhaks."

Next, he aimed an invisible rifle at them and pulled the trigger, imitating the sound of a gun report with his mouth. "You shoot men!" he said accusingly. Aiming his invisible rifle at the sky, he again mouthed a gunshot, and pointing to himself, said, "We shoot God." Then raising folded hands and stepping well within the personal space of the three men, who were staring at him as if he was berserk, he said in a forceful tone, "No violence! Shanti! Shanti!"

For a few tense moments, the Italian stared the three men down as if he was about to slug them all. Then he turned and began walking along the trail in the opposite direction we had intended to go. I turned and followed him.

We stayed on the trail until the three men were out of view; then we headed downhill and circled back to my cave. "I tell you I know these army bastards," he whispered. "They're a bunch of atheists. Arrogant atheists. You've got to talk their language."

We sat near the cave entrance and waited quietly, the stolen goods spread at our feet. I could only hope that the three men would not discover my cave. A minute later, they came tramping over the hill.

Reaching us, they turned, saw the cave, and with unabashed curiosity began heading towards the door. Again, my friend hopped up and stood in their way.

"I want to see your commander!" he yelled in the face of the one in charge.

The man seemed taken aback. "Commander?" he asked.

"Yes, your commander. Now!" he yelled, striking the palm of his hand with his fist. "You're bothering us. Harassing us. I want to report you to your commander. You don't know shanti, only war."

The face of the leader now flushed red with fury. His lips twitched. I was sure he was going to punch the Italian. Then one of the other men pulled on his elbow. They turned and slowly walked in the direction of town, looking back at us in cold suspicion.

How stupid could I have been to tell this wild man about my cave? Now the Indian army knew where I was, they had seen all the stolen goods sitting there, and they were mad. Who knew what they might do?

"Well, I think that did it," the Italian said in a tone of reasonable speculation. "I hope they don't come back. I don't think they will."

I picked up my pen and paper and wrote him a note: "I came all the way from the southern tip of India to this cave to do sadhana—alone. I came to live in a cave, simply, in silence. I appreciate your efforts, really, but I don't want anything to do with all this stuff you found. Please take it back."

He read the note. "Okay. I understand. I respect your sadhana, because no one has ever respected mine, so I know how it is. I'll just take these things and hide them until I need them. Will you help me carry them?"

I nodded.

We put the tins, plates, and rags in a nearby half-cave. "We'll store them here," he said, "but they'll be stolen by tomorrow. You'll see."

I already knew they were going to be "stolen," because as soon as he left, I was going to do it myself, and take them back to where they belonged.

We waited for a while to make sure the three men were gone, and then went to find the bed and pots. The bed was every bit as heavy as he had said. He wanted to throw it into the canyon, but I insisted we carry it with the pots back to the cave where he had found them. Reluctantly, he agreed.

After returning the bed and pots, I saluted him with folded hands and a friendly smile to show I had no hard feelings. With an abashed expression, he returned the salute. I felt sorry for him, but what more could I do? I walked back alone to where we had stored the tins, and returned them to Krishnadas's cave.

Finally, everything was back in its place. If the Italian wanted to steal them again, that would be his problem. Now I could only hope that my association with him would not result in another visit from the army, the police, or anyone else who might have seen our suspicious movements that afternoon.

It was 6 p.m. by the time I got to my meditation, exhausted and frazzled. Had it been a coincidence that the army showed up for the first time, just when my friend was in the process of robbing the caves? Is anything a coincidence? It seemed the energy the Italian put out attracted trouble like a magnet.

I sat to meditate before falling asleep, still feeling frazzled, while thoughts of regret filled me. How could I have been so stupid to go against my intuition? I never should have shown the Italian my cave. Then none of this would have happened. What if the army came back, in force, mad? It could be the end of my retreat. I could see no good coming from today, only bad. By trying to help the Italian, I had blown it completely.

To quell my fears, again I focused on meditation.

The frenzy of anxious thoughts didn't cease, but as I sunk into meditation, I began to feel a little distance from them. Then at one point, my mind shifted, and I saw my anxious thoughts in a different light: Weren't they only the futile, mad ravings of my mind? Truly, they were madness! Why fret about all the bad that *could* happen? What good did that do? If the army came and my retreat had to end, so be it. Perhaps that was what was meant to happen. I was only making myself miserable with my fears.

To hear the futile, mad ravings of the mind—to clearly perceive what a great noise they are—is to transcend that noisy mind. Transcending it, where do you go? Beyond the ego/mind, beyond fear . . . into the calm and sanity of Being.

Now I saw what a trickster my mind was. It told me that my happiness depended upon being undisturbed in my cave. But was that real? Did my happiness really depend upon that? Couldn't I still be happy if I were kicked out of my cave? Surely. I had been happy even before coming to my cave.

And there was something else I saw now: My attitude was that I should be able to stay in the cave, undisturbed. Why? Because that's what I wanted! In other words, life should meet my expectations. My expectations should actually control life. Clearly this was nothing more than a childish, mad raving of my mind. Life *doesn't* always meet my expectations. That's not how things work. Expecting life to bend to my will is a cause of frustration and misery because it simply is not the truth.

If an idea is true, it will help you to better get along in the world. This idea clearly wasn't working.

So what is the truth this situation was pointing me to?

Life may not bring what I expect, but it does bring Reality, always. Nothing more, nothing less. And that's how I grow, by learning to embrace what life brings instead of resisting it. When I accept what life brings, surrender to that, I align myself with Reality. Instead of fighting it, I move with life, embody life, the truth of what is.

Isn't that what it means to mature spiritually? To embody more of life, instead of childishly resisting life?

I thought of Christ's words, "I am the way, the truth, and the life . . ."* What could be higher than to simply embody life as it is? To outgrow childish expectations of bending life to my will, and *become* one with what is—the way, the truth, and the life.

Surrender and Be.

With this, the last vestiges of my mad ravings cleared. My thoughts ceased. My mind became still in an inner expanse of spiritual energy and peace.

After a while, the thought of the army came again. I felt no anxiety. In fact, I felt only love for them. So much so that this feeling took me by surprise—yet it felt entirely natural. They would do what they would do.

---

*   John, 14:6

They were an instrument of life, conscious or unwitting, delivering Reality. I had no control over them. I could only remain content in my Self. In that state of Reality, giving them love would be automatic. I could not do otherwise.

Reality and Love come hand in hand.

After finishing meditation, I wrote these thoughts in my journal. As I did, I prayed I would remember this. It seemed a great secret.

It also seemed to me that the entire day's events had been set up by God. Once more I had been shown that problems lie not in what happens to me, but in how I view what happens to me.

Listen for the mind's mad, futile ravings;
Recognize them and Be.
Life holds no problems—not a one.
All is a gift,
The cause of your liberation
From the mind.

I put aside my journal and continued to sit in meditation. My heart was now not only calmed, but I felt, at least so it seemed, as happy as a human being can feel. A sense of complete ease with whatever might happen filled me. Army or no army, cave or no cave, what matter?

A verse from Patanjali's *Yoga Sutras* came to me, and now I understood it for the first time.

*From contentment, unsurpassed happiness is gained.**

---

* Hariharananda Aranya, Swami. *Yoga Philosophy of Patanjali*. Trans. P.N. Mukerji. Albany, New York: State University of New York

CHAPTER 11

Devoured, Be

Offer yourself
Into that fiery mouth,
The fierce and merciless
All-Devourer.
Then discover;
The end of devouring
Is peace.

A few days later, my morning meditation went to a level that was more than I could handle. Just closing my eyes, the Infinite seemed to swallow my mind. Yet something was left of my mind, for though it dissolved into an unbounded vacuous space, it simultaneously jittered wildly with thoughts.

Press, 1983, II:42: 225.

Well, not exactly thoughts in the usual sense; rather, I can only describe them as the precursor of thoughts. Mental impulses that literally exploded before they could become thoughts, like drops of water bursting into steam on a red-hot skillet. My mind was hardly recognizable as a mind. Clearly, my process of purification had reached a feverish pitch.

After a couple hours of this, I stopped meditating and lay down. The relief was such that I felt I was floating in a blissful cosmic bath. I concluded I had all the Being I could handle. I was full. Overfull. I thought of seeing my wife and two daughters and my enthusiasm for leaving Gangotri peaked. By the time I left the cave to go to my meal, it was all over. It was time to go home.

Then a series of unusual events occurred. First, even though I was on time for my meal, the annakshetra inexplicably closed before I arrived, and I was left without a meal for the first time since arriving in Gangotri. I went to another annakshetra; they served me, but sparingly, and with suspicious looks that made me feel anything but welcome. I went for a bit more food to a cafe I had used now and then to supplement my daily meal. They happily served me, but shorted me on my change. When I mimed how much they owed me, though I was certain the owner understood me, he coolly ignored me.

Returning to the cave, I found that a large boulder had fallen into it and was lying on my meditation blanket. I had placed that boulder the second day after moving in to block a gap in the upper wall of the cave. It had seemed a bit unstable, but had lasted until that particular day. It seemed an odd omen.

Then that afternoon, as I was meditating, a tour guide came to my door and wanted me to get out—so he could show his group the cave. That was another first.

Aside from all this, that day I noticed that two unoccupied half-caves in the immediate area had been vandalized. Further, my money was down to just what I needed to get back to Kerala, my shoes had holes in the soles and my socks were getting wet, and that evening I ran out of honey and ghee. To top it all off, I hadn't been able to shake a flu bug and felt a sore throat coming on. It seemed the time to leave the heavenly abode of Gangotri had indeed arrived.

The next morning, in meditation, as soon as I closed my eyes, pure Being went on in my head like a light. The subtle energies in my body converged in my head, and the usual quiet blissfulness of meditation became much more physical and intense, almost orgasmic. Then my mind was forcibly sucked into an ocean of indescribably intense Being/light/energy/bliss. I disappeared; the world disappeared.

I have no idea how long I was in that state, but finally I emerged from it. Whatever force was in control of this meditation, however, wasn't standing still for that. A moment later, I was again sucked into that intense ocean of pure energy and light, and again I and the world disappeared. Once more, sometime later, I emerged. This cycle continued, over and over: waves of the ocean of Being-energy-light, moiling with the foam of ecstatic bliss, irresistibly washing away my conscious mind and individuality, as waves of the ocean wash away a castle of sand.

Finally, filled with electric energy and bliss, I lay down on my bed to come out of meditation.

How could I leave now? Yes, just a few hours earlier every particle of my relative self had wanted to go—to see my family, to write, to enjoy all the comforts of civilization—but now it seemed clear that those desires had been stirred only so they could be devoured and washed away by crushing waves of Being. I was now experiencing

Shiva-Being, the divine Destroyer, in action. If I really wanted my ego to dissolve into the Self, I could not but stay and let this almighty devouring force of evolution do the job.

At this thought, I felt a tinge of fear. Suddenly, it seemed a real possibility that I actually would disappear. What if I did gain enlightenment, and all I knew myself to be dissolved, never to exist again in the eternity of time? It seemed an even more final dissolution than death, for if the world's religions were right, at least after death, the individuality remains intact in either the afterlife or reincarnated on earth in another body.

I tried to reassure myself: What had been my experience over the past 26 years of meditation? Hadn't it been only of increasing joy, clarity, energy, creativity, and peace? Did such qualities lie in the direction of death, or in the direction of more life? As the scriptures put it, dying to the ego is to be born into one's true divine nature, eternal life. Hadn't Christ said, *"By gaining his life a man will lose it; by losing his life for my sake, he will gain it"?** My experience so far indicated a validation of the promises of the scriptures. How could I doubt now, just as the goal seemed to grow tangibly nearer?

Besides, why would I wish to preserve my ego? From all I had observed, in myself and in others, the ego seemed the source of negativity: arrogance, pride, selfishness, intolerance, self-deception, and anger. Less ego, on the other hand, correlated with more love, tolerance, patience, compassion, and graceful living. Wouldn't the complete absence of ego mean the dissolution of negative qualities, and the expansion of positive ones? Whatever disappearance of the ego at the moment of enlightenment

---

*   Matthew, 10:39

actually meant, it had to be for the best. In fact, it must be the supreme accomplishment of the finite ego to dissolve in the Infinite. I could not but trust in the perennial promise of the sages and the world's great scriptures.

Despite these elevated reflections, as I walked to town for my meal, ironically, the most trivial negative thoughts plagued me. I couldn't help thinking about the shop owner who had shorted me on my change the day before. The amount was the equivalent of less than a dollar, but it irritated me nonetheless, especially the shop owner's dismissive attitude. After a few minutes of quiet fuming, thankfully my thoughts shifted with a sudden insight:

Everything is a test. Every irritation, worry, aggravation, fear—anything that stirs a reaction of any kind— is nothing but a test. There is no meaningless or random irritating circumstance, no mere inconvenience or delay, no happenstance frustration of desire. All these are intricately and perfectly designed tests of one's integration of higher qualities, higher consciousness, into one's personality, heart, and mind. And our Tester, our loving Father/Mother/Beneficent Teacher, ever waits patiently for us to pass the test, for us to rise to our true Self.

In the next instant, I experienced the solution to my irritation with the shop owner. As my attention went to him, a part of myself melted in love and flowed to join with him. I felt one with him. He and I were the same; there was no difference between us—none.

I thought of the shop owner's happiness in receiving the additional money, and I felt his happiness as my own. I felt *his* happiness! That my personality located in my body had been the financial loser was irrelevant; his happiness was also mine, for we were one.

As I reflected on this more, I realized he might not have even experienced happiness over the event. Perhaps he didn't even know he had shorted me, or he might have even felt greed if he was in his lower self. Nonetheless, whatever his ego experienced, from the perspective of oneness with his higher Self, I could only experience pure delight and love at the very thought of him, for that was his inmost nature, as it was also my own. I could not but love him.

Previously, I had often attempted to live the spiritual ideal, "Love others as you love yourself," by trying, in a conflict, to see the other person's side, trying to imagine how they might feel. This is an important effort. Yet how much richer was this spontaneous experience of loving the shop owner as myself. I had no thought of his selfishness, only of his happiness, which I shared as my own. Loving him *was* loving my Self.

This experience gradually faded as I continued walking to town. Nevertheless, it left me feeling a resolve to never judge others. How can you judge someone harshly when you are one with them?

It does not matter what another does or doesn't do; never consider, even for a moment, their worthiness to receive love. Just give love, unqualified and unconditional. The moment you weigh the worthiness of another, you have fallen from love and truth. You have fallen from union.

In that afternoon's meditation, I experienced a peculiar sensation. I became aware of a tangible strength and solidity building, layer upon layer, in the tissues of my body. This was subtle, but clearly perceptible. It was as if I had been working out with weights for weeks, and now happened to see myself in a mirror only to find a new person—except this spiritual bodybuilding was invisible to others. No one would have been impressed by my pecs.

As I continued to observe this sensation, it seemed my body was actually being remade through the austerities and spiritual practices—transmuting into the unshakable, indomitable stuff of Being. I vaguely recalled that in his *Yoga Sutras,* Pantanjali, the famous, ancient exponent of Yoga Philosophy, declared that through austerity, impurities are destroyed, resulting in the perfection of the body and organs. Perhaps what I was experiencing was some aspect of this. Perhaps this build-up of spiritual energy in my body also related to the glimpses of higher consciousness that I had been experiencing, such as my unity with the shop owner earlier that day.

Indeed, just lately I had been feeling various changes—for one, a distinct emotional freedom, like an open-air space inside of me. This space teemed with a quiet joy, and brought an overall feeling of well-being and calm. It also brought occasions of spontaneous love simply at the sight of someone or at the sight of nature's beauty. Mentally, I had also been feeling clearer. In writing in my journal, inspiration and insight came more often and flowed more effortlessly. Intuitively, this layering of subtle energy, which must also involve chemical changes in the body, seemed to me the physical correlate of all of this.*

---

* Actually, this experience continues to this day, now some 20 years later. I came to recognize this spiritual energy as prana, life-breath

142

Perhaps this is why spiritual growth is such a gradual process: It takes time for the physical and subtle bodies to be transformed to support natural abidance in higher consciousness. When enlightenment comes, it may come in an instant, but how many years of patient culturing precede that instant? All layers of the body must be gradually prepared as a temple for the unbounded spiritual energy of the Self. Thus, we must be not only intent on the goal of realizing the Divine, not only make self-effort with intensity, but remain patient and surrendered to God's will.

How long have the Himalaya stood, patiently ready and waiting to whisper their songs of Being? How long has life been waiting for us to discover its Essence? This is the loving patience we, too, must show in return as we strive to realize the Divine. Learning patience is learning to surrender is learning to Be.

At one point during my meditation, the thought of Krishnadas came. I had not seen him and his sadhana buddy for over a week. Just a short time later, I heard footsteps outside. I opened my eyes and saw three heads peering into the cave—Krishnadas, his sadhana buddy, and the Swami who had translated for us last time. I waved them in.

---

being pushed into the nadis, or subtle channels, throughout the energetic body. This energy in turn invigorates, strengthens, and renews every cell in the body. On ajayan.com I teach specific techniques to accelerate this process. Also, see a discussion of the five sheaths (pancha koshas) in my book, *Effortless Mind: Meditate with Ease*: pages 78 - 80.

The three men entered all wearing rather dirty orange robes with thick wool sweaters. As they sat, I offered them food, but they declined. I offered water, and this they accepted. After he had taken a drink, the Swami who spoke English said, "Receiving even a little water from a sadhak, I feel myself blessed."

I felt unworthy of such a statement, but I envied his having been raised in a society that had cultivated so gracious a sentiment. Never in my life would I have had such a thought upon being given a drink of water. Raised in a secular society, I had missed such culturing and now had to work hard to develop spiritual sensibilities.

Now Krishnadas looked at me with soft eyes and began speaking in Hindi. I, of course, did not understand a word.

After a minute, Krishnadas paused and the Swami who knew English translated.

"Swami says that you are our spiritual brother, even though you are from a different country and culture. He invites you to stay with us and do sadhana together. You are a true sadhak and he invites you to live the life of a sadhu."

As the man finished, Krishnadas smiled warmly. I could not but smile back with appreciation for Krishnadas's love. Still, his suggestion was not very practical. I had a family, and my youngest daughter, Sudha, was only 8 years old.

Seeing that I remained unpersuaded, Krishnadas continued speaking to me directly in broken English. "Uh, our ashram, verrrry nice. Three meals, milk, tea, every day. You hut for sadhana."

I scribbled a note for the Swami who knew English. "Where is Krishnadas's ashram?"

"Punjab," he said.

With another note I asked for the address. After all, having my own hut might come in handy, for a visit anyway, someday . . . I rubbed my fingers together indicating money, and raised my palms in a questioning gesture to ask whether it was expensive.

"No, only little," Krishnadas said. For a few moments, he silently scanned the cave. Then pointing to the floor of the cave, he said in a definitive tone, "I stay tonight."

He meant to spend the night in my cave? Why? Perhaps he thought I was lonely living in the middle of the forest, or maybe he wanted to give me a taste of doing sadhana together, for he had told me that he spent much of each night in meditation. Krishnadas said a few more words and his buddy translated. "Krishnadas says he will leave now and come back at 7 p.m."

They left, but it rained that evening, and he did not come back.

As I continued my evening meditation, the significance of Krishnadas's invitation to be his sadhana brother sunk in. He was asking me to become a sadhu, just as he was, to renounce all, including family, to seek the Infinite in utter freedom. This was the third time he had made the invitation. Clearly he was not making it as lightly as I had taken it.

But no matter how serious he was, I knew I could never accept the invitation. I simply would not desert my family. Still, I had occasionally wondered if realizing the Self at some point requires renouncing everything in order to rub out the thick identity that hides the Self from Itself—to become no one's son, no one's father, no one's husband, not the businessman, teacher, writer, whatever. That is, to become, at least in some very significant sense, nothing. This meant you had eliminated the veils of ego that shroud the inner, divine Self.

Wasn't this what St. John of the Cross referred to when he wrote that we must "stand naked before God"?

The identities we normally and unwittingly wear must come off before we can see that God has already clothed us in grace, in the divine Essence that is at the heart of all.

But could adopting a different lifestyle actually be a direct cause of realizing the Infinite? It certainly was not sufficient cause: Tens of thousands of sadhus live a life of renunciation in India, yet it is generally accepted that precious few have realized the Self. How can realizing one's own Essence, which is said to transcend all boundaries, including lifestyle, be dependent upon a particular lifestyle? No, it seemed to me that enlightenment could not be gained by something so superficial as lifestyle. Yet it was also true that a major obstacle to knowing our true, infinite nature is that we become attached to things, people, circumstances, roles, and clothe our minds with identities.

All identities—"I am so and so's son or daughter, I am a parent, I am a writer, doctor, salesperson, I love nature, skiing, golf, I am a hard worker"—are but congealed thoughts of past and future. The past and future are filled with experiences that we hold onto as "I am this or that." The present is immediate. Nothing is congealed. The present is simply "I am."

Even the thought, "I will renounce everything, live a simple life dedicated to realizing the Self," implies an identity—"I am a spiritual person." This identity must veil the Self just as much as any other. So true renunciation is not selling everything and giving the money to charity, not becoming a wandering beggar.

Renunciation means only one thing: Discovering the Self in its original condition, prior to any and all definitions. This is the one, direct, cause of Being in the present. This is what it means to realize the Self. It is not a matter of lifestyle. It doesn't matter whether you work a 9 to 5 job or sit in your hut; your Self is untouched by this. You are like the infinite expanse of the sky, which may appear to embrace the earth, but is ever untouched by it.

"Stand naked before God,"
Shed the past and future
In which we clothe our minds,
And Be
One with He
Before whom you stand.

The next morning my stomach ached so badly I could hardly sit to meditate. I had been trying to ignore stomach pains for a couple of weeks, but for the past few days they had been getting worse. As I struggled to meditate, it struck me that the series of portents two days before must have indeed been the signal for me to go. It was time to leave Gangotri.

I had already said my goodbyes to everyone once. Since I was not feeling well, there was no need for that again. But there was one thing I had to do.

I had now been in silence for over two months. Before returning to the world, where I would be expected to speak, I had to end my vow of silence.

Where would be the best place to do it? Should I go to the shores of the sacred Ganga? Should I go to the top of the canyon where I had often meditated and contemplated the beauty of that sacred valley? Somehow it seemed right to do it right here, in my cave, where I had spent so many hours meditating.

I packed all my things, rolled up my sleeping bag and pad, and set it all by the door. I sat for a few moments with eyes closed. Then, in just a whisper, I began to chant a few Sanskrit prayers.

Om
Lokah Samastah Sukhino Bhavantu
Lokah Samastah Sukhino Bhavantu
Lokah Samastah Sukhino Bhavantu
Om Shanti Shanti Shantihi

May all beings (in the three worlds) be happy.
Om peace, peace, peace.

Om
Asato Ma Sadgamaya
Tamaso Ma Jyotir gamaya
Mrityor Ma Amritam gamaya
Om Shanti Shanti Shantihi

Lead me from the untruth, unreality, to truth, the real.
Lead me from the darkness of ignorance to the light of knowledge.
Lead me from death (this world of illusion and constant change) to immortality.
Om peace, peace, peace.

Om
Purnamadah Purnamidam
Purnaat Purnamudachyate
Purnasya Purnamaadaya
Purnameva Vashishyate
Om Shanti Shanti Shantihi

That is fullness (or perfect). This is fullness (or
perfect).
What comes from fullness is fullness.
What remains after fullness is taken from fullness
is yet fullness.
Om peace, peace, peace.

Om Brahmaarpanam Brahma Havir
Brahmagnau Braahmanaa Hutam
Brahmaiva Tena Gantavyam
Brahma Karma Samadhina
Om Shanti, Shanti, Shantihi

Brahman is the offering, Brahman is the oblation.
Poured out by Brahman into the fire of Brahman.
Brahman is reached by him
Who sees all as (the action of) Brahman.

Om Bhur bhuvah Swaha
Tat savitur varenyam
Bhargo devasya dhimahi
Dhiyo yo nah pracodayat

Om. We meditate on That transcendent Truth,
The Supreme Being, Who creates and illumines all
the three worlds.
Worthy of adoration, the divine effulgence, remover
of ignorance,

The resplendent Light and source of grace;
May He enlighten our intellect.

Even whispering required effort, and it took a couple of minutes before my voice could achieve soft speaking volume. Yet to my surprise, the cave echoed not just the sound of my voice, but a rich vibration of holiness. Suddenly, that little hole under a boulder, which had been filled with the palpable energy of meditation, now felt like a hallowed cathedral. The Sanskrit syllables had stirred the meditative silence and stillness into something even far richer and more sublime: the indescribable sweetness of Divine presence.

This experience recalled something I had once heard from a renowned Vedic pundit.* He had said that in the Rig Veda, speech is represented as a divine veena, a celestial sitar-like instrument played by Saraswati, the goddess of wisdom and presiding deity of speech. The Devi Veena's notes are said to stir and enliven the silence of transcendental Being and give rise to the entire creation, with all its richness and nuanced complexities.† That is, speech, vibration, stirs the unmanifest, infinite Absolute into something even more fulfilling—the wholeness of life, inclusive of both the entire active universe and the unmanifest Absolute. That wholeness alone fulfills the potential of the Infinite to express Itself.

This is mirrored on the level of human life. You cannot really gain complete fulfillment only by meditating. You need to be in relationship with life, with others, with

---

* The late, great pundit and scholar, Brahmarishi Devarat, said to be one of the few pundits of the 20th century who had committed the entire 10,000 verses of the Rig Veda to memory.

† Reminiscent of the conclusions of modern Physics, which sees all things as vibrating energy.

nature, yet also fully established in your own innermost nature, your higher, divine Self. *Living* this wholeness alone satisfies the heart, fills the mind, senses, and even the body with something so sublime that you know for certain there is nothing in heaven or earth to surpass it.

It seemed to me that those few chants had allowed me to briefly taste that nectar of the divine wholeness of life. I savored those vibrations of tangible holiness in the dank darkness of my cave for ten or fifteen minutes. Then I got up and walked outside.

Standing in the light of day, surrounded by the beauty of the valley, I was drawn now to go to my favorite spot, the canyon overlooking the Ganga. I made my way through the forest, savoring the smell of the deodars and pines, the feel of pine needles crunching underfoot, and the roar of the Ganga. When I had first arrived in Gangotri, that valley had seemed spectacularly beautiful, almost to the point of overwhelm. Now it seemed soft, so friendly; it was part of me, and I part of it.

I reached the canyon's edge and surveyed that Himalayan panorama. The teeming, milky waters of the Ganga thundered through the canyon, surrounded by pine-covered mountains and towering cliffs of reddish-brown stone. A thick layer of silver-gray clouds hung just above the highest peaks, and a cool wind beat against my face. A storm was coming.

I stood against the wind for a few minutes and cherished the power of nature, the power of that canyon one last time. How many hours had I sat or strolled there during the previous two months, enjoying nature's intricate beauty? Now my time here was at an end, and I might never see this canyon again. I lifted my pack, turned away, and began the trek to town.

Just as I walked up the last steps to the bus stand, the bus started pulling out with a shrieking honk, heading for Uttarkashi. I waved it down and climbed aboard.

As I stepped into the bus, my senses were assaulted by a cacophony of sights, sounds, and smells. It was jammed with pilgrims excited to be returning to their homes or heading on to the next holy place of pilgrimage. A group of old women in colorful saris were yelling at the driver about something and arguing with each other. Music blared from the bus's speakers. Cigarette smoke filled the air. The pandemonium was overwhelming.

I was content to stand, but an old man pointed for me to sit in the very back seat. Only so as not to refuse him, I scrunched in between an Indian army man and a boy at the window. A loudspeaker directly above my head blasted untold decibels of a high-pitched woman's voice singing Indian devotional music. In less than five minutes, I had a headache.

That bus was about as far from the peace of my cave as I could get, but somehow, despite my headache, I felt an inner evenness and silence. It was as if I were somehow separate from my body and the throbbing pain in my head. In fact, despite the physical discomfort, the depth and power of inner silence was exhilarating. The whole scene, my whole life for that matter, now seemed like a great play, filled with joy.

It is said that silence is golden. I felt like I was getting a lesson in that truth first hand—by the extreme contrast between the bedlam around me and the expansive silence within.

After fifteen minutes or so, at the first stop, the boy next to me got off. Now I had a window seat. Opening the window as wide as it would go, I put my head entirely outside. At once I felt free from the chaos of blaring music, loud voices, and cigarette smoke, and was back in the

Himalaya. I hung out of the bus the entire five hours to Uttarkashi, enraptured as the beauty of snowy peaks, forests, waterfalls, and the Ganga raced by. That sacred river could enchant me for hours with her exploding energy and tumultuous waves. Never had I seen anything quite so marvelous anywhere else in the world.

As the bus wove its way through the mountains, the thought came that I had not trekked to Gaumukh, the glacier that was the actual current-day source of the Ganga. This was something I had wanted to do. For a moment, I felt a twinge of regret, but then my regret dissolved into peace.

No, I had not seen Gaumukh; I had not traveled to the various ancient temples in that region; I had not climbed to hidden lakes or valleys carpeted with wildflowers. I had done practically no sightseeing whatsoever. Yet this Dev Bhumi (land of the gods) had filled me. I could not for a moment doubt that my little cave and that Gangotri forest had given me the very best of the Himalaya.

CHAPTER 12

Awakening the Witness

*Yogastah Kuru Karmani, "Established in Union, perform action."** This is the essence of all spiritual teachings. All else—commandments, worship, meditation, prayer, all spiritual qualities—are the outer expressions of just this: Be one with the Self and act, an instrument of the Divine.*

The bus arrived in Uttarkashi just before nightfall. The surrounding mountains, overgrown with jungle, stood silhouetted against a flaming, twilight sky. We were let off in the main marketplace—a motley jumble of small shops, restaurants, and fruit stands on both sides of a wide street, off of which branched several narrower alleyways, also lined with shops. The night air was balmy, at least 80 degrees, and filled with the smell of fried pakoras and

---

* *Bhagavad Gita*, II:48

papadams. The streets and alleyways were jammed with crowds of Indians shopping, eating, and browsing. It was the picture of convivial, summer nightlife in a Himalayan village.

I made my way through the milling crowd towards the same ashram on the Ganga I had stayed in on my way up. As it turned out, I got the very same room.

Never before had I so appreciated such a simple convenience as that room. The ashram was an old wood and cement structure and rather run down; on my way to Gangotri, my room had seemed dirty, dark, and dingy—barely tolerable. Now it was luxuriant. I could stand up straight without hitting the ceiling. There was a bed, and just to be off the floor seemed a glorious extravagance. For that matter, it *had* a floor. Though dirt and garbage from previous occupants was scattered under the bed, compared to my cave, the room was hygienic.

After a short set of asanas, pranayama, and meditation, I went out for dinner. As I walked through the alleys in search of a restaurant, I felt a surprising sensation—like I wasn't even walking, wasn't doing anything, was just abiding in an inner silence, witnessing my body blissfully stride along. This would become a familiar experience for me in the coming days. That inner silence, a blissful sun in my heart, created a felicity and ease. In meditations, I found myself sitting in this inner sunlight effortlessly. This was my first taste of the fruits of my meditations in Gangotri.

Finding a small, open-air cafe, I seated myself and was served. Halfway through the delicious North Indian meal, for no apparent reason (the cafe was nearly empty), the waiter seated a sweet, elderly Indian couple at my table. From their silver hair and weathered faces, I guessed they were in their seventies. In making polite conversation, I discovered they were on an extensive pilgrimage to the most important holy places of that area. They, too, had just been to Gangotri, and before that, Yamunotri, and were now headed to the Kedarnath and Badrinath temples.* They asked me if I would accompany them on the rest of their pilgrimage. When I said I could not afford it, they offered to pay my way.

Had I any inclination towards sightseeing, I might have accepted this generous offer. But I had no interest in pilgrimages other than to continue my inner pilgrimage to the Self. I felt it was either time to go back to Kerala, or—a long shot plan had already begun to stir in my mind—if the bank in Uttarkashi would cash my personal check, I would return to Gangotri. That is, if I could somehow heal my stomach. As politely as possible, I declined.

Nonetheless, the couple insisted I come to their hotel room. There they fed me delicious sweets until I could eat no more. Those sweets were a welcome treat, but the love of that winsome couple was the real nectar. They seemed nothing less than angelic messengers from God, greeting me on my return to the world.

The next morning, I set out to find help for my ailing stomach. I asked at a pharmacy and was told of an Ayur-vedic hospital, which turned out to be practically next door to the ashram I was staying in. The doctor there not only treated my stomach (successfully as it turned out), but refused any payment for the examination and medicine.

In retrospect, I realized that clothed in my weath-ered ashram white clothes and ripped sneakers—not to mention being thin, tanned, and bearded with over

---

*   This is called the char dham, the four seats or abodes. It is con-sidered a great blessing to visit all four sacred sites in one's lifetime.

two-month's growth—I must have appeared quite poor. Very likely I was mistaken for a sadhu, which perhaps also explained why the pilgrim couple had offered to help me the night before.

Then came the real test of grace: I went to the bank to cash my remaining traveler's checks and hopefully, to cash a personal check. The State Bank of India in Uttarkashi was a branch of my own bank in Kerala, so I anticipated that cashing my personal check would not be a problem. After being passed from one teller to another and finally to the manager, I was told that they could cash only my remaining Indian traveler's checks, not my personal check. Not yet equipped with computers, India's banks failed to honor deposits made even in their own branches.

The traveler's checks gave me 1000 rupees (less than $29.00 at that time). This would barely cover the buses, train, and hotels for my return to Amritapuri in Kerala. Not only could I not return to Gangotri, but I could not buy gifts for my family, and I might have to fast some of the way home.

As I walked out of the bank, I was disappointed, but accepting of what was to be. There was not much I could do about it in any case. As I walked back to the ashram, I happened to notice a computer school. I had brought a diskette containing a book I was working on, and I wondered if they could print it out for me so that I could work on it while traveling.

Inside the shop, I was greeted by a young man sporting a large, red turban and a long, black beard—a Sikh.* As it turned out, he could not print my document with

---

* Sikhs observe Kesh, the practice of allowing their hair to grow without cutting it. Thus, Sikh men have long beards and long hair, and wear a turban.

his software. We did, however, get to talking about my stay in Gangotri.

"Are you going back to Gangotri?" he asked me.

"No," I said. "I would like to, but I have run out of money. The bank won't cash my check."

"You need money?"

"Well, I think I have enough to make it back to Kerala."

"How much would you like? I will cash your check."

"No, that's fine. I can make it."

"Please. Allow me to help you."

He was so sincere, as was my desire to at least get a few presents for my family, that I could not refuse him again. "Well, five-hundred rupees would help a lot," I said, calculating meals, a few days stay in Rishikesh, and presents for my family that I could then buy. I had no intention of asking him for enough to return to Gangotri plus the return to Amritapuri, for that seemed like too much. Five-hundred rupees was less than $15, but I knew that for this fellow it must have been a week's wages, possibly more.

He gladly gave me the money, and we exchanged addresses so I could pay him back. Afterwards he told me, "I don't have very much money. In fact, I could barely afford that much, but whatever you would have asked for, I would have given, even if I'd had to borrow it. That is the way of the Sikhs; we live to help others."

At this I tried to return his money, but he would not accept it. Again, I was struck by India's deep and pervasive spiritual culture. God had certainly led me to the right shop.

The next morning, I caught a quick, dusty, and cheap shared ride in a "press taxi" to Rishikesh. Earlier that morning the taxi had carried newspapers from Rishikesh to Uttarkashi, and now it was returning. The rugged, jeep-like taxi was designed to seat 6; I shared it crammed in with eight others.

We flew down the winding mountain road. As the scenery raced by—mountains, flowering trees, and tropical jungle undergrowth—one particularly bright, lime-green rice paddy caught my eye. Enjoying its color and beautiful formation, I suddenly realized, *I AM this rice paddy.* There was no separation or difference between that field of rice and me. It was me.

Then I noticed the road ahead of us. *I am the road.* This was not a thought, but an obvious fact.

I became aware of the taxi. *I am the taxi.*

Then the thought of the distance between us and Rishikesh came, and I knew, *I am all this. I am this space; I am riding through me, to get to Rishikesh, which is me, to stay in a hotel that is me.* Just as a person ordinarily feels their body is "me," so each and every thing of which I became aware was clearly me. It was all my own body.

> *Only the sense, "This is my head, torso, legs and arms; I am this body," creates separation. When this identification with one's physical body dissolves, one realizes all things to be like parts of one's own body, for one's true Self, infinite awareness, is at the core of everything.*

Previously, I had thought that the experience of oneness extolled in scriptures in such terms as, "Thou art That," meant realizing oneness with the Infinite, the transcendent divine Self. Yet here boundaries remained—there was still a world of things—but it was clear that each and every thing I saw or thought of was me. This experience of unity lasted for about half an hour and then faded. Yet it left me filled with inner light, a powerful spiritual energy, and a feeling of great love and friendliness for everything.

After several more hours of riding scrunched between my Indian companions, we reached the outskirts of Rishikesh. I asked to be dropped off near a cheap ashram. The driver directed me to the Omkarananda ashram right on the Ganga.

I went inside and was greeted by a strikingly beautiful Indian woman in her 30s. I asked if they had any vacancies. With a gracious smile, she told me they did, and after checking me in, led me to my room.

I could not have asked for a better room. Modern and immaculate, it offered an unobstructed view of the milky-white Ganga, which here flowed languidly. Unlike the cold and cloudy weather in Gangotri, in Rishikesh the sun was hot. Standing on my balcony in the sun and watching the huge expanse of water flow slowly by, I felt surrounded by warmth, comfort, and peace.

I had checked in for three nights, which qualified me for a lower rate on my room. This would also give me time to see Rishikesh and strengthen my body with some good food. Now that my tapas was over, I was constantly hungry, and as it turned out, ate ravenously every day I was in Rishikesh. Even the simplest foods tasted ambrosial.

Though I appreciated my room and the view, and savored the delicious food, I noticed the peculiar sensation that my mind was unmoved by these pleasures. This took no effort or discrimination on my part. There was no virtue of self-discipline in it. Rather, my meditations in Gangotri had simply created a built-in detachment.

This was a wonderful and exhilarating sensation: Enjoying everything, yet feeling greater satisfaction in the inner silence accompanying and underlying the enjoyment. It seemed a taste of what the *Bhagavad Gita* describes: "When he withdraws the senses from the sense objects, as the tortoise its limbs, then he is firmly established in pure consciousness."* Previously I had thought this verse to apply only in meditation, but now I saw it could also apply even during activity with eyes open.

Noting such changes in my inner experience only again sparked my desire to return to Gangotri. My stomach was already feeling better from the Ayurvedic medicine. If I had gained so much from two months in that cave, why not see what more could be accomplished? With such thoughts, though, often came another interesting experience.

A faint feeling would spontaneously arise: *But I already am.* It was as if pure Being (the eternal silence of infinite pure awareness) momentarily bubbled up into my mind, and I felt I was That. Then my constant hankering to "achieve enlightenment"—which I was usually so identified with—seemed insignificant, unnecessary, and misplaced. *I already am . . .*

Ironically, this phenomenon, which seemed to me a first budding of "witnessing" (a state described in India's scriptures as an aspect of living higher consciousness) also sometimes occurred when I reacted negatively to something.

One time a motor rickshaw driver grossly overcharged me; another time I ordered a veggie burger without onions, and was served a veggie burger that not only had onions on it but was completely made of onions. Both times I reacted with irritation. Yet it was actually my negative reaction that seemed to shift my awareness. Suddenly, I found myself witnessing my own reaction, yet feeling that the irritation did not touch "me" at all. To onlookers I appeared just one more frustrated Westerner traveling in India, but on the inside, there was no me to be frustrated.

---

*   II:58

There was only an inner, silent awareness, witnessing the experience of frustration without being moved by it.

This felt freeing. Previously, when I would react negatively, it would reflect on myself and create a subtle sense of inadequacy. It implied a flaw in my being: I lacked patience, or equanimity, or love. Yet now it was clear that no reaction, however unwanted or negative, could sully the true me—that inner, shining sun of pure peace, of simple awareness.

Thoughts of regret might even still come: "Oh, I shouldn't have said that," or, "I shouldn't feel this." Even feelings of inadequacy might still come, but these thoughts and feelings seemed to play out on the surface of my mind. Like the reactions of anger or irritation, they failed to obliterate the inner sunlight of the Self.

Still, this left the question: If I was really free, why was I not spontaneously embodying spiritual virtues, like patience, love, and compassion? Why did I still have so many apparent faults? An answer came:

Though your pure, transcendent nature may shine within through spiritual practice, the transformation of the personality takes much more time. The personality is gradually molded to express higher qualities in the crucible of everyday interactions and experiences.

Still, it seemed to me that the opening of inner awareness would help in this transformation of the personality. Ordinarily, we are so identified with our thoughts and feelings—we are so flush with them—that we have no other perspective to guide us. We live blindly to a degree, bound by our thoughts and feelings, much as animals are bound by their instincts. Yet it is usually easy to see how another person is caught when they become angry, frustrated, or neurotic. What if you could view your own behavior as if it were another's? Wouldn't that help you mold your behavior?

This is not the same as the psychological state of dissociation. There is no defense mechanism in the face of stress. Quite the opposite. Witnessing allows you to become more aware of yourself and your thoughts and feelings. It is not the mind thinking about itself or trying to observe itself; it is awareness—the *heart* of the mind—shining in its pure and simple state, free of identification with the mind and body. Old patterns of thoughts and feelings still arise, but in the witnessing state, they seem small compared to the peace and expansiveness of the inner, unbounded Self.

One other aspect of witnessing I noticed: You begin to glimpse your Self as the heart or silent core of everything. That is, in looking at scenery, people, or traffic, for instance, I would sometimes feel myself—simple, invisible presence, underlying the seeing of the eyes and mind—as if spread to underlie everything. You see what you are—silent awareness—everywhere. And in this recognition, you begin to feel a natural empathy and love for all.

This reminded me of Christ likening the Kingdom of Heaven to a mustard seed. That inner, pure awareness, which is pure joy, the heaven within, is "tiny" (even atomic) in that it is hidden. In uncovering That, you shed layer after layer of what is apparent—"I am not the body, not the mind, not these feelings or thoughts, not the sense of 'I'"—to find what underlies these: simple awareness. In this process, you proceed to what is smaller, or subtler, to the atomic, and even beyond. Yet that same hidden seed of awareness deep within is then found to underlie and pervade everything. It is smaller than the smallest, but also Cosmic, all-inclusive, infinite—the atomic mustard seed that becomes greater than the greatest, the kingdom of heaven.

This awakening is the seed of real transformation. For with this sense of unity, of natural and spontaneous sympathy and love for everything, a new possibility dawns: For the personality to be recreated by love, by the freedom and fullness of simple awareness.

One final thing I noticed about witnessing: On occasion, it seems this awareness of underlying unity allowed not only the witnessing of my own mind, but occasional glimpses of witnessing the minds of others.

On my second day in Rishikesh, I was shopping for a gift for my eldest daughter's birthday, which I had missed. In one shop with many brass statues, I found a small statue of Kali (the fierce form of divine feminine). I really liked the statue, and I knew my daughter would love it, but it was far more than I could afford.

"You like it?" the handsome young Indian shopkeeper asked.

I nodded, but marked on it was a price of 800 rupees. No way could I afford that.

"It's more than I can afford," I said.

"For you, only 600 rupees," he said.

I shook my head. There was no way I could spend that much on a gift, as much as I would like to. "That's still too much," I said.

I continued to examine the piece. Normally, I would be too timid to offer a small fraction of the asking price, but I really liked it. I decided to take a wild stab, even if he laughed at me.

"I can only afford 100 rupees," I said.

The young shopkeeper, a very friendly fellow who seemed sincere and honest, broke into a wry smile and shook his head, "No, sir. I'm sorry. Even my cost is more than that. This is a fine piece. Just look at this work, all handmade. You won't find another piece like this in all of Rishikesh."

As I looked at him, I saw he was lying. I was certain of it. Now this in itself is no proof of anything. Any savvy buyer (I later learned) would know that of course he was lying; that's the name of the game. However, not only was I *not* a savvy buyer, I knew he was not telling the truth because I had felt it in his mind.

"This is not a handmade piece," I said.

He shook his head with dismay at my cynicism and put the statue back on the shelf behind him. Perfectly calculated to arouse guilt in me for not trusting him.

"Okay," I said. "I'll keep looking around for something else," and I started to walk out.

At this, he caved. "Okay, wait. Come back," he said with a motion of his hand.

"You are a very good negotiator," he said, looking at me with his charming, friendly smile.

He pulled out a scale and weighed the piece. (Years later another shopkeeper would tell me that almost all the shops bought their statues by the kilo, for very cheap. Apparently, none are actually hand crafted, but are caste en masse and sold by weight.) The statue weighed just under a third of a kilo.

"150 rupees," he said.

That seemed more reasonable. I assented and happily watched as he wrapped the statue in old newspaper. My daughter would love it.

For me, such instances of witnessing the thoughts of others were entirely random, but this reminded me both of Amma, who had often shown to me that she knew my mind inside and out, and also Maharishi, who once not only read my mind, but the minds of hundreds of soon-to-be TM® teachers at once. Not only did he read our minds, he instructed us on the purely mental level, without saying a word. It was an interesting experience, so I'll relate it here.

This occurred back in spring of 1973 in La Antilla, Spain. Some two thousand men and women, all meditation enthusiasts, had gathered on the southern coast of Spain with Maharishi to be trained to teach meditation. I had been there for 6 months, meditating 8 to 10 hours a day. It was the last night of the course and we were all gathered together in a huge tent on the beach. Maharishi was giving us final instructions, answering questions, and generally delighting the crowd with his sweet, playful, wise, and loving presence. The meeting went well into the wee hours of the next morning, when someone raised their hand to ask one last question.

"Maharishi, you haven't checked our mantras yet. Could you check them?"

The questioner was referring to the set of mantras that Maharishi had given each of us individually over the few previous days. It was from this set of mantras that we would select a mantra to give when instructing a person in Transcendental Meditation®. This was the main reason we had traveled to Spain: to study with Maharishi to learn to teach meditation—and the mantras were a key part of the process. We had been told that before the end of the course, Maharishi would meet with each of us individually to make sure we had the correct pronunciation of all of the mantras. With such a large group, however, this had not yet happened. Now here we were, about to leave for the airport, after spending up to 6 months here, and we had not yet had our mantras checked. For many of us, at least, it was a critical situation.

Seated on a couch on the stage, surrounded by flowers, Maharishi chuckled and surveyed the room with the two thousand expectant would-be teachers. "How many need to have mantras checked?" he asked in his sweet sing-song Indian accent.

Instantly nearly everyone in the room raised their hands, including myself. I thought I correctly remembered their pronunciation, but I wasn't absolutely sure, and this was too important an issue to leave to guesswork. I would have hated to give out mantras for years to come that were incorrect. I imagine most of the others in the room felt the same way.

Maharishi laughed. Raising his hands in a gesture of helplessness, he asked, "What to do?" Clearly it seemed an impossible task. People would have to start leaving for their flights in a couple of hours. Maharishi continued to look over the assembly for a few moments. "Let's meditate," he said simply.

We all closed our eyes in meditation. A few minutes into the meditation, I was surprised to hear an inner voice say each of the mantras. I immediately recognized the pronunciation of the mantras to be what Maharishi had whispered to me in our previous one-on-one session. I was also surprised to realize that in the interim I had indeed changed and distorted their pronunciation.

A few moments later, Maharishi ended the meditation by saying, "Jai Guru Dev," his way of passing on to his teacher all credit for anything he did.

Once everyone had opened their eyes, Maharishi again surveyed the room. "So now it's clear, eh?"

There could be no doubt he was letting us all know that what we'd received in meditation was correct. The same fellow that had asked originally again grabbed a microphone. "But Maharishi, will you please check our mantras?" Apparently, he hadn't gotten the message.

Maharishi chuckled and again surveyed the room. "How many still need mantras checked?"

At first only a few hands went up. Then a few more. Then more. The more hands that went up, the more doubt seemed to sweep the room, until almost everyone had again raised their hand. Finally, I raised my hand, too, though I felt a twinge of shame, because I knew I had just received the mantra check in meditation as surely as if Maharishi had whispered them in my ear. Still, if everyone else was going to get a check, I figured I'd better too. I would hate to start teaching with any doubt of the mantras. Besides, another personal contact with Maharishi was hard to pass up.

Maharishi chuckled heartily and quickly organized a mantra check for those who wanted it. We lined up. Sure enough, when it was my turn, Maharishi whispered the mantras in my ear exactly as I had received them in the group meditation. As I left him, he gave me a knowing smile that had the effect of removing any lingering shame I had for joining the ranks of doubters.

Whereas my witnessing of another's mind was far from under my control, full mastery of this and other abilities naturally unfold to master yogis. Again, Amma had demonstrated such abilities so frequently that those around her hardly registered it as unusual at all. Nonetheless, it was encouraging that I was starting to glimpse this possibility. This also sparked my desire to return to Gangotri, to continue my sadhana and hopefully complete my quest.

Yet I had barely enough money to return to Amritapuri. How could I possibly return to Gangotri? So, the day after arriving in Rishikesh, I accepted the inevitable and took a motor rickshaw to nearby Haridwar where I bought a train ticket for Delhi to Kerala. The earliest reservation I could get left in three days.

Returning to my ashram room, I began to meditate. The face of a friend at Amritapuri, Scott Chase, flashed in my mind's eye. I thought nothing of it, other than as an indication of my immanent return to Amritapuri and anticipation of seeing Scott there. I continued meditating.

After a few minutes, I heard the sounds of rowdy play in the gardens outside my room, and from the voices, I could tell it was a young Indian boy and an American man. The boy's voice I recognized. It was a young beggar the ashram I was staying at had adopted off the streets when the boy's parents had died. The man's voice also sounded familiar. I tried to place it: Was that Scott Chase? But surely it could not be him . . . So I continued meditating without looking outside.

That evening, as I ate dinner at a nearby restaurant, I overheard a tall American man at the next table mention the name Scott.

"Excuse me," I said, "did you say, 'Scott'?"

"Yes."

"Not Scott Chase by chance?" I asked.

"That's right."

"He's here? Do you know where he's staying?" I asked.

"He's at Omkarananda ashram."

That was where I was staying. How could this be?! Not only was Scott in Rishikesh, nearly 2,000 miles from where I'd last seen him, but there had to be at least twenty or thirty ashrams in town. We had picked the same one!

I returned to the ashram, got Scott's room number from the man at the desk, and knocked at that door. A moment later it opened, and there stood my friend. "Ajayan!" he nearly yelled. After mutually amazed greetings, he invited me in.

Scott is an affable, down-to-earth, longtime meditator. He is tall, solidly built, with a cherubic, bright countenance that gives him an air of innocence. At one time, he had spent a couple of years in a monastery in preparation to become a monk. We had very much enjoyed what little of each other's company we had shared over the past few years.

"What are you doing here, Scott?"

"I was in America on tour with Amma and decided to come here for a break before jumping back into the fire at Amma's ashram. What about you, Ajayan? What happened to you? You look like hell!"

I told him about my stay in Gangotri.

"That sounds amazing," he said, and a light went on in his eyes. "You wouldn't want to go back up there, would you?"

I had known that it would take a miracle for me to be able to return to Gangotri. Here it was, in the form of Scott. He offered to lend me the money I needed to buy new tennis shoes and supplies and to get up to Gangotri and back to Kerala afterwards. It seemed sheer grace. How could I say no to such a miracle? And how could I deprive Scott of the experience of meditating in Gangotri, for he made it clear that he would not go there without me.

That night Scott and I made our plans, and the next day we caught a motor rickshaw to Haridwar to refund our train tickets and buy supplies for our return to Gangotri. We decided we would cook for ourselves in Gangotri. Now that Scott had lent me money, we shared expenses equally, and we spent a lot, at least by my standards.

In retrospect, if I had any regret about my return trip to Gangotri, this would be it. Practically without noticing, in the time I would be with Scott, I would spend exactly three times per day what I had spent while alone.

In truth my regret was not really the money, which was not that significant by Western standards, but that our relative extravagance subtly changed the tone of our trip. When I was alone and spending almost nothing, there was a sense that I was relying on God's grace. To make such a trip without money leaves you no option: you *have to* rely on grace. Living by faith, and the tests and austerities that follow, only deepens your relationship with the Divine. As a result, your *spiritual* wealth increases. Conversely, with money, you can hardly but rely upon your pocketbook and yourself—money is so practical, and it works so well in the world. Having plenty of money creates the illusion your ego is in charge. You're perfectly capable of taking care of things, which appears, superficially at least, to remove the Divine from the equation.

For this reason, as long as money is in the hand, the Divine tends to remain a distant ideal more than an operating principle in daily living. Perhaps this is why Christ said, "It is easier for a camel to pass through the eye of a needle than for a rich man to enter the kingdom of God."* Rather than bring your fortune to India, how much more appropriate and humbling on a spiritual journey to live simply and travel lightly, taking refuge in the Divine.

Be that as it may, once we'd purchased our abundant supplies, which included not only plenty of food, but a pressure cooker and even a rope (for which I had special plans), we caught a press taxi bound for Uttarkashi.

---

* Matthew, 19:24. India's scriptures do prescribe the way for a rich man to enter the kingdom: offer your ego to the Divine by giving generously in charity, without ostentation or pride, with gratitude for life's bounty. Giving a significant portion of what we hold dear is a sacrifice that can be just as transforming and humbling as traditional renunciation (giving everything away at once and becoming a wandering mendicant). This is the path prescribed by India's scriptures for those living in society: enjoy material and spiritual success through gracious charity.

CHAPTER 13

Fire of Knowledge

"I am Brahman" is not an egotistical statement. On the contrary, its true meaning is that there is no "I" left, just Brahman. "I am Brahman" is the ultimate expression of selflessness, the limit of humility. You have disappeared and only the Infinite remains. "I am Brahman. I am the light, the way, the Truth." No ego can say this honestly, only the Divine, the complete absence of ego. You could as easily say, "I am nothing."

From Uttarkashi, we caught a bus the same day for Gangotri. It was well after nightfall by the time we arrived at Gangotri's bus stand, which I had left only a week before. The ramshackle huts and shops on either side of the road, with campfires burning, felt like home. I was back! The miracle had happened.

We stepped off the bus into the chill mountain air, thick with the fragrance of burning cedar. After retrieving our gear from the top of the bus, we crossed the footbridge over the river and started walking through the forest towards my cave. It was dark, so we lit our way by flashlight. I could not resist pointing out, with great ebullience, all the attractions so familiar to me—a waterfall here, an overlook there, a patch of sorrel to add to our meals—even though we could hardly see any of it in the dark. All the while I just prayed my cave was still empty. As we neared it, we became quiet and crept up to the small wooden door in the darkness. I peeked in. It was empty, just as I had left it.

We unloaded our things, built a fire, and cooked some rice and mung beans in our new pressure cooker. It felt like camping—a different experience for me than living in the forest alone, with full focus on my spiritual practices. I knew that Scott wanted that experience, and I didn't want him to miss out on it. That meant we'd have to live in separate caves and observe silence. We talked it over and Scott agreed, enthusiastically in fact.

I told him of the cave the Italian had found down on the beach of the Ganga, almost straight below my cave. The Italian fellow had said it even had a store of firewood. That sounded like our best bet for a second cave—riverfront, view property, too. Scott was excited, and so was I. The only catch was getting down there. For that I had specifically purchased the hundred meters of 1/2-inch nylon rope. With it, I figured we would be able to easily climb down to the river and up again.

That night we both slept in my cave. The next morning after meditation, we headed towards the Ganga to find an ideal home for Scott. My plan was to descend to the river down the same rock slide that I had discovered before, only this time with the help of the rope.

Cautiously, we made our way down the wet and slippery goat trail until we reached the top of the rock slide. Surveying the drop to the river, Scott looked dubious.

"Ajayan, are you sure about this?"

"No, but it's worth a try," I said.

"Okay, you try, I'll watch," he said.

"Fine." As a youth I had climbed many a cliff. Besides, climbing up and down ropes was fun and good exercise.

We doubled the rope and secured it around a large pine growing at the edge of the cliff. Then we tied knots in the doubled rope so it would be easy for me to hold on to. Keeping my feet on the rock slide, I lowered myself hand-over-hand down the rope to the grass ledge. I reached it safely. Nothing could have been easier. Now, with rope in hand, I calmly surveyed the 30-foot drop from the ledge to the beautiful, white sandy beach below. If this worked, Scott would be living in paradise. I described it to Scott and told him that I was going over.

"Ajayan, you're crazy!"

"No I'm not," I returned, exasperated by his utter lack of adventure—and it was going to be *his* cave, too.

I threw the rope over the ledge, firmly grasped it, and started to lower myself over the lip. As I continued to inch lower, the sinking feeling came that perhaps Scott was right; this might be a big mistake. But how would I know without trying? Pushing my apprehension aside, I shoved myself away from the ledge and found myself dangling in mid-air, thirty feet above the ground.

Under my full weight, the rope stretched taut—as thin and hard as steel wire. I could barely hold on. Even the knots didn't help. The rope slipped through my hands, tearing and burning them with agonizing pain. My instinct was to let go of the rope to save my hands, but I knew that could mean a broken leg or worse. Instead, exerting every ounce of strength and will, I grasped the rope more tightly, allowing it to slip through my hands as slowly as possible. Painfully, I lowered myself until I was within a few feet of the ground. Finally, I let go and tumbled onto the sand.

My hands were rope-burned, and all the buttons had been torn off my shirt, which had gotten caught in a knot in the rope. Otherwise I was okay.

"Ajayaaan! Ajayaaan!" Scott had been yelling down to me the whole time.

"Yeah, I'm down," I yelled back, "but I don't think we can do this on a regular basis."

"Can you get back up?" he yelled.

"No," I shouted back. "Not by the rope. I have to find another way. You go make breakfast for us, and I'll meet you at the cave."

I could hardly believe it. The canyon had gotten me again—or my recklessness had. I examined the cave the Italian had told me about. It was not a cave, but a massive overhang of white rock sheltering an area about twenty yards long and fifteen feet deep. It would have made an absolutely beautiful (albeit freezing) home—if only it were accessible. Someone had indeed stockpiled a supply of firewood under the overhang, so there had to be a way up. That had been my one ace in the hole: I knew that if the Italian could get down and up (and he had said it was an easier way than my rock slide), then I could do the same.

I made my way upstream along the Ganga to search for that easier way. It was a different world, untouched, solitary, and beautiful. Brown and white cliffs towered above me, studded with gnarled pines. Lining the edge of the rushing river were immaculate sandy beaches and white boulders. Here and there, flowering bushes and ground cover had been masterfully placed by a divine hand. It was a magical garden, a paradise—just me and the Ganga.

For all its magical beauty, however, there was no possible ascent upstream—only a hundred-foot, overhanging rock cliff straight down to the water. I headed downstream.

Here, too, I found no viable way up, just more unscalable cliffs. How could that be? The Italian had done it somehow. But then he was a climber, and crazy.

I sat on a boulder. I couldn't actually be stuck, could I? The possibility loomed like an ominous cloud. No, I simply had to find a way up.

Upstream was clearly impossible, so the way to the top of the canyon had to be downstream. I looked again and found one slim chance—a vertical climb up forty feet of rocks and dirt that looked virtually unassailable. Above that was forest but on a very steep slope. That was where I had turned back when the Italian had tried to lead me down to the river. From this vantage point, it was clearly absurd the Italian had tried to lead me down that way. He was worse than crazy.

I contemplated my alternatives. I could wait. Scott would finish making breakfast and come to see what was taking me. I would yell for him to get help, and probably he could get the army to come for me. What would they do, carry me up? Raise me by a rope? Not only did that option seem humiliating, but I really didn't want anything to do with the army. Besides, then they'd again see my cave. No, I had to climb out.

Anxiety gnawed at the pit of my stomach. I dreaded climbing that cliff. As a child, I had experienced no fear of heights whatsoever. I would climb tall trees and jump from one treetop to another. Even occasional falls had failed to instill either good sense or trepidation in me. Then about college age, I had developed a mild fear of heights for no apparent reason. Over the years, I had worked against this uneasiness, standing on the edge of cliffs and tall buildings to overcome it, but those were situations where I was in control, and safe. Here, neither was true. I had already seen how here nature ruled, and that any sense of control I might have is illusion. Here there was good reason to be scared.

For all this, I felt a slight sense of witnessing my fear—some inner calm, despite the same familiar fear response in my body that I'd felt for years over heights.

I found the most likely route, took a deep breath, and began my ascent, looking for handholds and footholds among the rocks and dirt.

As I climbed, at several points I was unable to go straight up; then I had to figure out which way to go, left or right, before proceeding. It was an unwelcome taste of what I imagined real rock climbing might be like. By sheer grace, I managed to get almost to the top of the first 40-foot cliff. Almost. I clung to the cliff with an outcrop of dirt and rock blocking my passage further. There was nothing to hold onto either left or right. I was stuck.

Up to this point, I had focused only on going up, ever watchful for the next handhold and the easiest route. Now, for the first time, I made the mistake of looking down. A shot of panic passed through my body like an electric jolt. I was much higher than I had imagined. The rapids of the Ganga roared beneath me. If I slipped and fell, my body would be broken on the rocks below.

The sense of witnessing deserted me. Trembling and breathing in short gasps, I hugged the cliff more tightly. I had done it again. My life was hanging by a few clumps of dirt. Worse, my fear was almost paralyzing. I felt dizzy. In my panic, it seemed that an invisible, sinister hand was physically pulling me to fall to my death.

Barely resisting the destructive grip of my fear, I breathed deeply and concentrated with all my might on the dirt in front of my face. This calmed me enough that I could think again. Going left or right was impossible. Even if I could muster the courage to climb back down, I would only have to climb up again. It seemed I could not go up, but I had to.

I prayed to Amma. She had answered my prayers before, so I could only hope. I was desperate. No witnessing, no unity now; I was her humbled child. I prayed for thirty seconds as hard as I could, to make sure she heard me wherever she was on her world tour. Then I took another deep breath and began to climb. Managing to get my left foot higher, I shifted my weight onto it and raised myself perhaps a foot. In that awkward position, barely hanging on to the cliff, I reached above the overhang and desperately felt the ground for a handhold. My fingers touched a thick root that looped out of and back into the ground in the shape of a perfect, solid handle. *Amma, thank you!* Pulling myself up by that root with all my strength, I scrambled onto the top of the overhang.

From there I faced what would have been another difficult climb, except that a fallen tree was dug into the ground right in front of me. Its trunk rose up the cliff with stumps of branches all along its length—an ideal, natural ladder. *Amma!*

By the time I got to the top of the canyon, I looked like I had fallen down several cliffs. My shirt was torn wide open, my face, hair, chest, and clothes were all smeared with dirt. Yet I felt entirely blessed. I was alive! Unsteadily, I walked in the direction of my cave, breathlessly thanking the Divine and Amma with each step. This time I had really learned my lesson. There would be no more foolhardy explorations for me.

I found Scott hunched over a fire. Breakfast was almost ready.

He looked up and seeing my condition, stood up straight. "Gaaawd, Ajayan! What the hell happened to you?!"

"Don't ask. But we need to find you a different cave. That one's out."

The rest of the day we spent setting Scott up in a small cave close to mine that I had found in my previous explorations. It needed some work, and it wasn't river-front, but it would do. We officially initiated our sadhana and began observing silence.

The next morning, as I began yogasanas and pranayama, I felt like a hunter, a hunter of Being, who had returned to the hunt.

Yes, the Self must become a full-time pursuit. The hunt must extend even outside of meditation, and become all-consuming, one's whole life and one's full attention devoted to That. One-pointedness is everything, until the Self shines in the heart eternally, effortlessly. Only then does the chase stop.

As soon as I closed my eyes to meditate, I was plunged in a crystalline ocean of consciousness. It seemed that no longer was meditation a matter of meditating; rather, it was sitting in Truth, and That, so simple and pristine, was more fulfilling than anything I had experienced before.

Meditating is only a means, a preparation. You medi-tate only so long as you are in the dark, for all spiritual experiences that come in meditation—bliss, light, whole-ness, seeing forms of the Divine, unbounded shakti—are just that, passing experiences. They come and go. They are relative. The Self, Truth, remains hidden.

To sit in Truth, so simple, so entirely normal, one with the ocean of Being, is to care nothing for spiritual experiences. They become insignificant. Spiritual experiences may purify the heart and mind, they are necessary for a time, but eventually you see they are passing and of little consequence. They are still darkness, or at best, rays of light in the darkness. You want only to be that Truth of all things, to become the Light itself.

Over the next couple of days, though, the inner burning of purification again returned, and I realized something else: He who would hunt the Self, soon becomes the hunted. This time, however, it seemed there was a different angle on the purification.

Streams of "pure knowledge," as forceful and rushing as the Ganga herself, coursed through my mind. They were not knowledge about anything in particular, nor even thoughts, but rather, currents of inconceivably powerful, pure attention. It was the opening of my mind to an entirely new level.

Just as immense, atomic energy underlies the apparently inert objects of the world, so within the ordinary mind lay awesome power—atomic attention with the coherence of a laser, the vastness of space, and the energy of the sun.

It seemed to me that if the power of this pure attention could be channeled with skill, anything would be possible. Perhaps this was the power behind the legendary yogic supernormal abilities, the *siddhis,* such as levitation, invisibility, and the like.

Insights also came, but only when the force of that atomic attention diminished; when it was in full force, I could not think at all. Thinking while immersed in that awesome stream of attention would have been like trying to swim while submerged in the rapids of the Ganga. Yet I was aware that those streams of pure attention held a kind of knowledge nonetheless. This gave me a new perspective on the purifying power of sadhana.

All you know yourself to be is a tremendous complexity of information—biological information, past experience, instinct, desire, habits, and so on—all coded into each and every cell. Your life is a crystallization of information. The pain of purification arises during intense sadhana because divine knowledge, the knowledge of the Self— pure, untainted, and immortal—tears apart that relative, conditioned information of which you are made. It all must be purified, made transparent, in order for you to live in the light of absolute knowledge, which sees nothing as other, but all as Self. This releases the soul from eons of conditioned and inbred fear, into absolute peace and love. It also expands ordinary human capabilities to the supernormal, the miraculous.

My first spiritual teacher, Maharishi, had said that to gain enlightenment, even the DNA of every cell had to be completely purified. At the time, that tidbit of understanding flew right over me. Now, I felt I was discovering it for myself. Every cell of the body must be transformed—and pure, absolute knowledge, the basis of living in divine union, does it. As Krishna says in the *Bhagavad Gita,* "Indeed, no purifier like knowledge is found in the world; he who is accomplished in yoga, with time himself finds this in himself."*

The purifying power of this absolute knowledge seemed to open a door to unlimited transforming possibilities. In this vast, beautiful, mysterious creation, Truth includes everything, not only Zen-like simplicity, but the richness of divine love, the sublime holiness of the saints, the spiritual energy and grace demonstrated in the lives of Christ, Buddha, and others. Within the infinity of possibilities, even the physical body may be divinized.

Both Hindu and Buddhist lores, for instance, refer to the possibility of transforming the body into a radiant form of pure light. Tibetan Buddhists refer to this as the *jai-lus,* the "rainbow body." The Vedic literature refers to the possibility of achieving a body made of the light of consciousness, and fantastic longevity, through austerity and prolonged meditation. Kishore had told me he had seen beings meditating upstream from Gangotri with such bodies of consciousness/light.

Unfolding such possibilities requires a highly advanced state of purity, sufficient solitude, the appropriate intention, and detailed knowledge of specific advanced practices. It seemed to me that the atomic power of Truth into which I had tapped opened the possibility of just such a transformation—though I had yet to discover the precise means.

Despite all this fantastic potential, to sit in Brahman is to know that the Self is above and beyond all possibilities. Nothing can ever touch That. Nothing can add to It. Physical longevity, a body of light, these are hardly significant in the face of the simple fact that one's own Self is ever free, absolute, the very source of all, and utterly fulfilled.

---

*   IV: 38

May a full moon shine
Blissfully
In your mind.

The next day was Guru Purnima, the Hindu celebration honoring the guru, which falls on the full moon of July each year. For those who have imbibed the nectarous grace, wisdom, and love flowing from a true guru, this day is perhaps the most sacred of the year. In the morning, I performed several mental pujas* to my teachers. That afternoon Scott and I went to see Dineshananda.

As we approached the saint's hermitage, we were surprised to see the usually quiet ashram abuzz with activity. In fact, Dineshananda sat surrounded by no fewer than 20 or 30 disciples. Scott and I looked at each other, uncertain whether we should crash the party. I really wanted Scott to meet Dineshananda, and I was sure Dineshananda wouldn't mind, so I urged Scott on with a wave of my hand. As we came closer, Dineshananda saw us. He broke into a radiant smile and immediately called Kishore, who thoughtfully brought a pad and paper for us.

"This is my friend, Scott, also from Amma's ashram in Kerala," I wrote.

Kishore translated to Dinesha, who smiled and gave both Scott and I some Indian sweets.

"Guru Purnima?" I wrote, and with a wave of my hand indicated all the guests.

---

* A puja is a ceremony of worship or reverent remembrance.

Again, Kishore translated to Dinesha, who told us that not only were they all there to celebrate Guru Purnima, but the next day he, Dineshananda, would leave for a one-month pilgrimage to circumambulate Mt. Kailash, the legendary abode of Shiva.

This surprised me. Dineshananda seemed so comfortable in his remote Gangotri ashram; I could hardly picture him traipsing around a huge mountain at high altitudes for a month straight. Why would he ever want to do that?

I nodded to show I understood.

Dineshananda said something to Kishore to translate to us.

"'It is for my devotees that I go.' This is what Dineshananda wants me to tell you," said Kishore.

So, he had read my mind. Through Kishore, Dinesha continued to make small talk with Scott and I. He saw to it that we had plenty of food, especially desserts, and generally made us the celebrities of the day.

I didn't know it then, but I would not see this saint again until years later, and then his arm would be paralyzed, and his body wracked with pain from debilitating diabetes. (He would have to cut short his pilgrimage around Mt. Kailash, too.) Yet he'd have the same smile and glint in his eyes, and the same child-like joy would be shining from his face. A few more years later, on a subsequent visit, I would ask for Dineshananda and learn he was bed-ridden in an ashram in Haridwar, living out the last of his days. Later that year, I would learn from a friend that Dineshananda had died. The Swami at Krishnashram would explain to me that diabetes had taken Dinesha, that his "blood had turned sweet from lack of exercise and eating the desserts devotees constantly brought him." But now this cheery saint sat in front of me, glowing with innocent wisdom, an embodiment of joy.

That night Scott and I continued our silent celebration of Guru Purnima by walking into the forest to a wide plateau of smooth, white rock overlooking the Ganga. The plateau, surrounding mountains, and forest all glistened in the otherworldly light of the full moon. Scott began to meditate, but I could not close my eyes. Instead, I watched the brilliant lunar jewel slowly rise between two mountains. Moving gradually south as it rose, it appeared to roll up the side of the southern mountain. The illusion was perfect. Scott eventually opened his eyes and watched it too.

For nearly an hour, the resplendent orb rolled up the mountain's side to its peak. Since sitting even a few hundred yards in either direction would have skewed the perspective, that divine illusion had an audience of just two—Scott and I. It was a miracle, for us. The Divine's personal gift to enjoy on that sacred night honoring the fullness of the guru.

That night I was awakened by rustling in my cave. It was the same rustling that had disturbed my sleep almost every night since Scott and I had returned to Gangotri. We had been keeping our food in a bucket in my cave, and nocturnal foragers apparently regarded this as an invitation. They rattled and rustled through the packages of food, munching and making a racket, but I had yet to see what kind of creatures they were.

Figuring it was time to draw the line, I picked up my walking stick and flashlight and crept in the dark over to our food. I turned on the flashlight and with my stick walloped the plastic bucket that contained our goodies.

A moment later a large mouse (or a small rat) climbed out of the bucket and plopped onto the ground. He took a few uncertain steps towards the wall of the cave. My blow had stunned him. It would have been easy to do him in then and there, but I didn't want to hurt him (in fact, I hoped I hadn't hurt him); I just wanted some undisturbed sleep.

Then the strangest thing happened. The mouse turned and lifted himself onto a large rock directly in front of me, making himself completely vulnerable. Crawling to the rock's edge closest to me, he faced me, bent his forelegs, and bowed his head down to his paws as if prostrating; then he slowly raised himself and lifted his head to look at my face. For perhaps 15 seconds he looked at me with large, soft, unblinking eyes. Finally climbing off the rock, he crawled into a crack in the cave's wall.

I could hardly believe what I had just seen. What an amazing creature! A circus trainer could not have trained him to do better. Was this perhaps some yogi, reincarnated as a mouse for a sin committed in a past life? Whatever the case, from that night on, whenever my pious little roommate woke me up, I just rolled over and let him eat his fill.

CHAPTER 14

Cosmic Tsunami

Being teems with the pure potentiality of unlimited pos-
sibilities from which the entire universe springs. Experi-
encing I am That pure potentiality brings inconceivable
bliss.

When Scott and I came to Gangotri, we had no idea how long we would stay. Our romantic fantasies were to stay for months, meditating in our caves, return-ing to Amma's ashram enlightened sages. As a practical test, however, Scott vowed to take ten days of silence to see how it would go. By the end of the first week, he was already showing signs of discontent. It was August, the heart of the rainy season, and it was cold, wet, and alto-gether miserable. Worse, his cave leaked and the dripping sound kept him awake.

We had agreed upon the need for private space, so neither of us were keen on sharing my cave. Still, I knew the gracious thing to do would have been to offer to trade caves with Scott. Perhaps the cold and wet would still have discouraged him—or not. But I had grown attached to my hovel. Humble as it was, it held so many memories, as well as the energy of countless hours of meditation. I was really attached to it—and I knew it.

At the time, I felt more than a twinge of guilt for not offering Scott my cave. Now, 20 years later, though I understand the attachment I felt back then, I see this was by far the greatest single missed opportunity of my retreat. I only wished I had taken it—by graciously offering Scott my cave. This would have been a sign of maturity, of having integrated some of the grace I'd received. I know now that this integration is the real and most meaningful challenge of spiritual growth. Sadly, I did not see this then.

Such is the tricky nature of the human mind. To undergo the trials of living in a hole under a rock for the purpose of spiritual growth—only to become attached to that hole! I imagine whatever divine beings witness our actions must either have a good laugh or shake their heads in dismay at such behavior.

Dineshananda had actually warned me of this. As he said, you must find that peace wherever you are. If you think you'll find it by renouncing the world and retiring to the mountains, you will only become just as attached to the beauty of the mountains, forest, or river—or to the vibrations in your cave.

What is the real mark of progress on the spiritual path? I am convinced it is turning this natural human selfishness inside out into selflessness—a way of being whereby you graciously give without expectation of return or thought of self. Now, years later, I see that meditation alone cannot create such a change. Meditation has many wonderful benefits for health, happiness, vitality, mental clarity, and opening consciousness. It is a great tool that can help you live your creative potential joyfully. It also gives you a much broader perspective by expanding awareness beyond the ego, to the witness state. But becoming selfless seems to require more than this. Somehow, we have to break the deeply ingrained pull towards our own ease and comfort, rooted in attachment to the body. This attachment is the source of selfishness.

Perhaps, over years of life experience, that selfishness and attachment lessens if you really strive to overcome it. One classical technique to do this is to purposely give to others what you would want for yourself, even when it means a sacrifice of your own pleasure, comfort, time, or other resources. St. John of the Cross expressed this eloquently:

> *Endeavor to be inclined always:*
> *not to the easiest, but to the most difficult;*
> *not to the most delightful, but to the harshest;*
> *not the most gratifying, but to the less pleasant;*
> *not to what means rest for you, but to hard work:*
> *not to the consoling, but to the unconsoling;*
> *not to the most, but to the least;*
> *not to the highest and most precious, but to the lowest*
> *and most despised;*
> *not to wanting something, but to wanting nothing:*
> *do not go about looking for the best of temporal things,*
> *but for the worst,*
> *and desire to enter into complete nudity, emptiness, and*
> *poverty in everything in the world.*[*]

---

[*] St. John of the Cross. The Collected Works of St. John of the Cross. Trans. Kieran Kavanaugh and Otilio Rodriguez. Washington, D.C.: Washington Province of Discalced Carmelites, ICS Publications, 1973: 102 - 103.

Yes, this passage conveys the self-denial that characterized monastic life in his time. Still, considering the difficulty of freeing yourself of selfishness, his insight in suggesting a practical path to selflessness is wonderful. It directly counters the ego's attachment to its own comfort and pleasure. Even applying yourself just a little to this practice would help soften the grip of selfishness. Had I been as committed to this practice as I was to meditation, I would have insisted Scott have my cave—and experienced a breakthrough in integration. In that sense, I missed out.

We had only been in Gangotri nine days when Scott scribbled in his notepad that he was going to leave in time to be in Amritapuri for Amma's arrival. That meant he would have to leave sometime within a week. Now I had to decide whether I would travel with him or stay. Though we had come to Gangotri together, we had no expectations that we would necessarily leave together. We both understood it was an individual decision.

Ever since first coming to Gangotri, the date I would return to Amritapuri had been a mystery. What would be the signal telling me to finally return home? Would it be an intuition? Sickness or an accident? The first snow of the season? Would lightning have to strike my cave to get me to leave this heavenly abode? I didn't have a clue, and so I had always pushed the question away, figuring I would know when the time came. Now, with Scott's decision to leave soon, I could no longer avoid the issue.

Leaving was anything but an uninviting prospect. The thought of my family brought a yearning to see them. Amma was returning from her world tour August 18, and it would be respectful to be there when she returned. Besides, I knew I could not be on retreat indefinitely. What I had gained in Gangotri could not just be hoarded for myself; it had to be given in the service of others with love, or it would be of no use to me or anyone else.

Still, with all I had experienced lately, the perennial pull to stay in Gangotri remained. The same thoughts came: I had yearned for such a retreat for 30 years. When would I have another chance like this? Perhaps never again in this lifetime. Now, however, these thoughts were less compelling than they had been. They seemed somehow stale, as if they were past their prime.

Then in my morning meditation, I recalled something Amma often says: "Meditation is like gold, for it leads to realization of the supreme Self. Yet if we can express divine love and compassion in our lives, then we become like gold that exudes a sublime fragrance."

She was certainly an example of such fragrant gold. Recalling her constant, unflagging giving of herself, I suddenly felt that I had my signal. I knew when to leave Gangotri and return to Amritapuri.

To give of yourself selflessly is meditation in action. That is beyond meditation with eyes closed.

Emerging from my cave, I found Scott already preparing our meal. I scribbled a note telling him that I, too, would return in time for Amma's arrival. I had steeped in the Self for over two months. Now it was time to apprentice under the master of love, and to give of myself to my family and others, to give something of what I had received in this sacred place.

My decision pleased Scott. We further decided that before we left, we would take a one-day trek to the actual source of the Ganga, Gaumukh, the glacier from which the Ganga flows at almost 13,000 feet.

There is no you
There is no me
Just the Self
Shining
Eternally.

In that afternoon's meditation, the shakti in my mind and body seemed almost overwhelming. My body literally vibrated with spiritual energy coursing through it.

Occasionally, some eager new student of meditation has asked me, "How can I awaken *Kundalini Shakti?**" But they have no idea what this really means. They would open the floodgates, in their own body and mind, of the cosmic energy that creates, sustains, and destroys the universe. To experience this is completely unlike anything in ordinary life.

Say you are an experienced surfer who has surfed all over the world. You have ridden the best and biggest waves.

---

* Kundalini Shakti is the creative potency of the Absolute that generates the universe and dwells within each human being in their root chakra. Awakening that energy so that it rises and opens the chakras, in a natural, unforced way, is conducive to enlightenment.

One day you are out floating on your board waiting to catch a good one. Suddenly you see a wave forming a half-mile out. As you watch the wave approaching, it becomes huge, rising to the height of an eight-story building, and it is traveling unbelievably fast, a mountain of rushing water. With a shock, you realize what is about to hit you—a tsunami!

The power of that mountainous wave is far beyond anything you have ever known—on another order altogether—but you don't have any choice; you are too far from shore to do anything but try to ride it. That is approximately what you may feel when that cosmic energy, an aspect of your own inner Self, awakens fully. When it does, you can only hold on for dear life and hope that you come out of it in one piece.

That morning the tsunami hit my cave. It felt as if my concentration became so piercing that it split an atom in my mind. My head was filled with intense energy, as if my mind had become the sun, yet this was subtler than any physical energy. It was THE energy that had created all suns. It was awareness, crystalline in clarity, blissful, and extending throughout the universe.

The word, "cosmic" expressed this state of awareness perfectly. It was of cosmic proportions—all inclusive, vast, encompassing the entire universe—and it was consuming my mind.

After perhaps forty-five minutes of sitting in that state, I knew that it was too much for me. Not only did the familiar baking feeling come, as if I had a high fever, but it seemed that my body might possibly explode.

Then came the thought:

Shakti, like everything else, is nothing other than the Self.

With this, my awareness relaxed into that cosmic power. I merged with it, or it merged with me—and the unbearable intensity dissolved into peace. I had been guided to the secret of riding the impossible tsunami of cosmic energy.

An ego can no more contain cosmic energy than a surfer can ride a tsunami. The only way is to dissolve. Become nothing.

Boundaries alone create discomfort and intensity; when there is no boundary, no ego, there is only peace. The tsunami smashes any solid object that it hits, but it passes through air without causing any damage. To put it another way, become nothing and you become the tsunami of cosmic energy, which is then instantly revealed to be the perfect peace of the Self.

This is ever the secret of meditation: Continually dissolve anything and everything—the object of every thought, any perception, the awareness of he who is meditating and the process of meditation. What is left is just the pure existence of the Self.

Now, instead of unbearable power in my body, I felt a steady stream of calm and soothing subtle energy flowing up my spine and filling my head. In fact, in the days that followed, I would often become aware of this, even outside of meditation. This peace, this subtle energy, this sweet empowering fullness, held my awareness in an integrity and calm.

I also noticed that from that day forward, after merging in the tsunami of cosmic power, meditation was characterized by sitting in a deep silence that evenly permeated everything. And though my body felt calm, it was also filled with immense power, especially my head. This power was as tangible as my body itself; it was the power of the cosmic tsunami, only no longer wild. The tsunami of cosmic energy had been tamed, or rather, integrated.

The overriding sensation now was not of power, but rather of simply feeling much more normal, more at ease, and more balanced than before. I felt more myself. I noticed that during the day, just walking in the forest, or doing my yoga asanas, I felt so balanced and at ease; peace and felicity flowed constantly through my whole body. It seemed to me that if someone were to suddenly feel this, they would be convinced they had received a wondrous miracle. Indeed, it was a miracle, though that miracle had required a lot of sitting.

Another thing I noticed was that now my experience of the world with eyes open was dominated by silence. Everything was held in silence, within me, and around me. That silence is peace, stillness. All that happens in the world, the rushing of the Ganga, the wind blowing through the trees, walking through the forest, people talk-ing and laughing in town—all of it takes place in a field of silence.

I could not help but wonder, "Does silence really underlie everything, or is this only an altered state I am experiencing?"

The silence of Being is like the stillness of the arrow fully drawn on the bow; it brims with hidden potential energy. Without that stillness, the arrow is lifeless. With it, the arrow can fly.

This holds true for everything. Every subatomic parti-cle in existence must have as its foundation a bed of stillness and silence—pure, unmanifest potentiality. Otherwise, it would have no potential, and having no potential, could simply not exist. On what basis would the subatomic particles vibrate? Like the arrow that is not drawn back on the bow, they would be dead and without activity. They would cease to exist.

Everything is the expression of dynamic silence. The basis of everything—which is ever moving, changing, in activity—is silence. And it is within the range of human experience to live that silence pregnant with cosmic energy.

This recalled a talk I had heard in the early 1970's by a physicist. He was drawing parallels between the conclusions of modern quantum physics and reality as experienced in higher states of consciousness through meditation. In particular, he had compared the quantum field vacuum state to the state of pure awareness or transcendental Being. I could not recall the details of his talk, but he had said that quantum physics calculates that all sub-atomic particles manifest from the quantum field vacuum state, an abstract nonmaterial field of pure potentiality.

Physics may mathematically identify the abstract silence upon which all activity in the universe is based as the quantum field vacuum state. Yet the finest instrument of perception, the human nervous system, can be developed to experience that pervasive silence directly. And that silence, the Essence of all, is indescribably sublime and sweet, all-powerful, pure, the source of all. It can only be described as Divine.

That day, lying down after meditation, I was caressed within and without by silence. My entire body was drenched in blissful, golden streams, as if my blood had turned to a golden liquid dispensing pure joy.

Again, I recalled the saying, silence is golden. This now took on a new meaning for me. The human nervous system can be developed to directly experience the Silence that is *literally* golden. Someday, perhaps Western science will measure how that experience transforms the nervous system and biochemistry.

It was the day before Scott and I were to tackle the trek to Gaumukh. An hour or so into my afternoon meditation in my cave, thoughts of my Western sadhu friend, the Italian, came to mind. I had hoped to see him again before leaving Gangotri, but it looked like that was not to be. I had not seen any sign of him in town.

Though I had expected to meditate until bedtime, I felt an impulse to lie down and come out of meditation, which I did. After a few minutes, as I lay on the floor of my cave, I heard footsteps outside. Opening one eye to peek through the cave door, I saw a tall, thin Western man approaching with a backpack on.

"Hari Om!" he called out.

It took me a moment to recognize him, for he did not have his orange dhoti and shawl on; instead, he was dressed in a plaid shirt and jeans. It was the Italian.

Pushing open the door to the cave, I joyfully saluted him with joined palms and waved him in. As he sat, I wrote him a note saying that he could have the cave in three days.

"Looks like I came back at the right time," he said with a weak smile.

He appeared to have lost a lot of weight. I mimed to him that he looked thinner.

"Yeah. I'm reducing my food," he said. "I talked with a homeopathic doctor in Delhi and told him I wanted to cut my food to nothing. He said he would try to help. He gave me some pills to prepare my system, but he was cautious. Mind you, it's an unusual request," he added, squinting at me knowingly. "Anyway, I've quit grains and dairy; legumes will go next, then vegetables. I hope to be down to pine needles soon." He smiled with a haggard expression. "But traveling was hell, and I'm suffering now."

I wrote him another note: "I hope you'll be careful. I was thinking it might be better not to spend the winter here. It would take a miracle for you to survive."

"Oh, I've decided not to," he said. "It's not worth dying over. Besides, someone gave me a downer." He patted his pack. Noticing my puzzled look, he explained. "A sleeping bag filled with goose down—the real thing. You don't get warmer than that. They cost over five hundred dollars. I've got a Walkman, too. I don't feel safe leaving all that in a cave. Some bastard would steal it for sure. I won't spend the winter here without a hut that locks. In the meantime, I'll work on reducing my food and cloth, and I want to get my sleep down to a couple of hours a night."

The irony of his certainty that his things would be stolen from a cave made me smile. He was in fact the only person I had encountered in my stay in Gangotri that had actually stolen from a cave. Yet, somehow, in that moment, the Italian's paranoia seemed endearing.

I wrote him a note saying that I was going to Gaumukh the next day.

"Going to Tapovan?" he asked, with raised eyebrows.

I shook my head no. The walk from my cave to Gaumukh and back was 40 kilometers roundtrip. That was plenty for me in one day. Tapovan was a further steep climb of several more hours, and that would mean spending the night there, which I didn't want to do.

"It's *cooold* in Tapovan," he said. He shook his head slowly, and his face screwed into a look of distaste. "The wind cuts right through you. No trees up there either. It's bleak. I went there once, and it wasn't a good experience. I went to Mataji's."

This aroused my curiosity. I had heard of Mataji. Several friends of mine had gone to see this holy woman, and she had impressed all of them. Supposedly a true Self-realized saint, she had lived in Tapovan at almost 15,000 feet for many years. She freely invited people to stay in her cave with her during the warm season. During winters she stayed in her cave alone, snowed in for 6 or 7 months, unable, I had heard, to even see the light of day. Someone had told me, however, that she had just that year suffered some medical problems and was now in a hospital in Haridwar, and that she would never be able to return to Tapovan. With a questioning look, I encouraged him to continue.

"I got there at dinnertime," he said. "There were a lot of people with her. They had a full *thali*,* with rice pudding for dessert. It had cashews in it, and real milk. I couldn't believe it! How they got real milk up there is beyond me," he said, shaking his head.

"Anyway, I sat down and they didn't serve me. I was hungry. I wasn't eating much back then, so I was skinny and totally wasted from the climb. After a few minutes, I motioned with my hand to my mouth for food. 'Can I have some, Mataji?' I asked. Then the fellow next to me, an old monk with about three teeth left, sticks his head

---

*   An Indian meal consisting of a variety of dishes, served on a round, metal platter.

right in my face and starts laughing." The Italian imitated the fellow, bouncing his head up and down and laughing like a goofy cartoon character, "'Yuk, yuk, yuk, yuk . . .'

"He was so obnoxious that I picked up a thali plate and hit him on the head with it. The next thing I knew, they were all over me, hitting me with kitchen utensils—ladles, big spoons, whatever they could get their hands on. A couple of army guys that were there broke it up. I was half-conscious, scratched, bruised, bleeding, and one of the army guys tells me, 'You have to go down, you can't stay here.' I just mumbled, 'Yeah, go down.' I could barely stand up. They gave me dinner though, and then I left. Anyway, I don't really care much for Tapovan. It's too damned cold."[*]

We continued talking for a while (that is, he talked, I mimed and wrote notes). Finally, we wished each other good luck and farewell. As he walked off, a lonely figure, slowly disappearing down the trail through the pines, I realized that I had never asked his name. Nor had he ever asked mine. Neither had he ever heard me speak a single word. Yet I felt a bond of friendship with him, and I would not soon forget him.

My work is His,
Any talent I have is His,

---

[*] I later did meet Mataji. She had indeed suffered from arthritis from the cold and had to move to a lower elevation where she did charitable work for the poor.

200

Any fruits that come are His;
I am nothing but a vessel, an instrument.
All is His
And that is supreme joy!

That night after getting into bed, I meditated for a while, and in the midst of meditation came what seemed a vision of my future. I was no longer married to my current wife. Yet I was happy. I was much older and teaching meditation and leading retreats. I was no longer living in the ashram either.

Some of this was not surprising, but some made me feel sad. No longer married to my wife? I decided not to judge it or give it too much credence. I would, after all, only know for sure if what I saw was true when it actually happens. So there was no use in fretting about it. But it had appeared vivid and real. In any case, the mechanics of the possibility of seeing the future seemed apparent—if what I saw was true.

Once the mind becomes purified and freed, even temporarily, from attachments and desires that give rise to ordinary thoughts, you may glimpse the future. For this to happen, you can have no investment or desire in the seeing—no attachment, worry, excitement, none of this. Seeing the future must be a clear, clean, objective seeing, and you must let go of the vision as innocently as it came.

You will also know that any pride or gratification in having seen the future may alter the future seen—inevitably for the worse, for the influence of ego, even subtly, is always for the worse. Best to allow that vision to remain in the state of innocent consciousness in which it came.

In this was evident another principle as well:

To realize your highest dreams, live fully in the present. In the present, you can act and create. The present is ever the most precious opportunity, which alone leads to the highest future.

Far more important than any detail I may have seen of my future that night was the sense that the Divine plan is unfolding in the perfect way, in the perfect time. Our lives are a tiny part of that plan. Everything—all opportunities, our work, our play, the fruits of our labor—is not ours. The Infinite takes care of all, in a timeline that is not ours to control. We must make our efforts, we experience free will, we are self-determined, but ultimately the Divine accomplishes everything. This is the great paradox and gift of our lives.

CHAPTER 15

The Final Tapas

*Realizing the Infinite
Is not difficult
Nor is it easy,
It is nothing you do at all.
Your own, innermost Self,
You have never been anything else,
Nor will you ever be.*

*Nowhere to go,
Nothing to do,
Beyond all,
Like the hollow at the center of the seed.
"I am That I am."*

*Still, the path is its own.
Reaching his destination, the traveler rests.
Who, seeing this, would say,
"Ah, so resting is the way."*

At 7 a.m. Scott and I set off for Gaumukh. At the far end of the valley where we were headed, the first light of dawn silhouetted snowy peaks against a deep blue sky. We had lucked out; it was going to be a clear, sunny day.

The trail into the mountains was well-traveled and ascended gradually through a wonderland of coniferous forest and Himalayan views. Excited by the adventure before us, we started off at a fast pace. I kept the lead. The air was crisp and fragrant with pine, the early morning peace broken only by the song of birds and the crunch of our footsteps on gravel.

Though the trail was well groomed for the most part, it was also a test of grace. The elderly couple that had fed me sweets in Uttarkashi had told me they would never take it, for they considered the path to Gaumukh extremely dangerous. Now I saw why. Much of the trail passed under ominously towering overhangs of loose rocks and boulders; one tremor, and good-bye pilgrims—which at the moment meant us.

After about 7 kilometers, I began to tire. Despite the fabulous views, walking steadily uphill at that altitude took its toll on me. I just couldn't get enough air to feed my muscles to keep up the pace. Scott overtook me. Another hour passed and now only with great effort could I walk fast enough to keep him in sight. Sitting in a cold cave for two months, ten to twelve hours a day in *padmasana* (full lotus position), was hardly appropriate training for such a hike.

Sometimes the trail narrowed to just a couple of feet. Then we inched along to avoid the sheer drop of hundreds of feet straight down to the roaring Ganga. A couple of times, we had to cross over makeshift bridges of logs thrown over places where the trail had caved in. But the beauty surrounding us, and the excitement of our quest, dwarfed any fear.

About noon and some fifteen kilometers into our hike, we reached Bhojbasa—a few tarps on wooden frames that served as tea stalls and a large guesthouse on barren, rocky tundra. We were now well above the treeline, and from here, we had the first unobstructed, distant view of our goal: a huge, bluish-white wall of ice. This was the Gaumukh glacier, from under which flowed the Ganga. The massive ice wall seemed only a half-kilometer away, but this was an illusion created by the barren landscape and the gargantuan proportions of that ice face. We still had five kilometers to go.

As we neared the glacier, we passed a group of eight or nine tea stalls set up along the trail. This was the desolate outpost of Gaumukh at about 13,000 feet. The stalls not only served tea, but also offered bedding to any hapless pilgrim who actually thought to spend the night. In several of the stalls, exhausted pilgrims huddled under blankets, protected from the cold and gusts of wind that blasted us with fine sand. By this point I could barely stand, but the grim prospect of joining those pilgrims for an overnight stay spurred me on.

Now the trail brought us to within a few yards of the Ganga. Ice boulders—small, large, some as big as cars—lay strewn around the landscape. Other gigantic chunks of ice floated downstream, shaking the earth as they thumped their way down the rocky riverbed. Limpid ponds of crystalline, turquoise water covered large areas of ice and snow. Silence permeated the place, accented by a faint whistle of frigid wind. The stark, icy landscape was another world, unlike anything I had ever seen.

As we negotiated the final turn around a rocky hill, the face of the glacier came into view once more. It rose perhaps 70 feet, a sheer, jagged cliff of dirty, bluish-white ice. Out of a large cave in the middle of its base emerged the milky waters of the Ganga.

For a few moments, I studied that ice cliff. Here began India's holiest of holy rivers, revered for thousands of years, a river of legend and myth, on whose banks unnumbered seekers had ardently sought and achieved their highest spiritual goal. How many *pujas* (ceremonies) had been performed on its banks? How much devotion had its life-giving waters stirred in the hearts of India's people? How many bodies of saints had been laid to rest in its currents?

I suddenly felt dizzy and sat on a boulder to steady myself. The trek had utterly exhausted me. Despite the significance of the moment, I was in no condition to fully appreciate it. I rifled through my pack for food, found some cheese and crackers, and scarfed it down to quell my hunger and hopefully regain some strength. Meanwhile, Scott, who was in fine shape, took off his shirt and began giving himself a ritual sponge bath. Ice boulders floated by, passing within a few feet of him, but he seemed unfazed by the chill of the elements.

We had planned to return to our caves that day, for neither of us wanted to spend the night in that freezing desolation. But that meant we had just an hour or so to spend in Gaumukh lest we run out of daylight on our descent.

After eating I stripped down and stooped behind a boulder to dip into the icy waters. It was even colder than in Gangotri, but a couple of months of daily baths there had prepared me for the worst. It actually felt refreshing to my aching muscles.

I dressed and decided that there was one more task I had to do before starting the long trek back to Gangotri: I had to actually touch the glacier. Then I could really say that I had been to the source of the Ganga. After all, I had not come from the southern tip of India to *almost* get to the sacred river's source.*

I surveyed the wall of ice before me and the large ice cave from which flowed the milky, icy waters of the Ganga. At the mouth of the cave, piles of ice formed a convenient walkway out to the center of the river. I suddenly had a brilliant idea: Scott had brought a camera. He could get a shot of me standing on that ice walkway in the center of the river, just inside the ice cave. What a fantastic picture that would make! I mimed to Scott to get his camera ready. Then I set out for that walkway.

No sooner had I taken my first few steps, when a block of ice the size of a pick-up truck broke loose from the top of the glacier. With a thunderous splash, it sent a six-foot wave and a gushing spray over the ice walk, exactly where I was headed.

Okay, scratch the walkway shot.

Still, I figured I could at least touch the glacier. Probably that ice falling was a once-in-a-year occurrence; we just happened to be lucky enough to see it. As I continued towards the glacier, though, several more huge ice blocks broke loose and fell, creating a spectacular show. With those massive chunks of ice crashing down so near, it seemed the end of the world had arrived.

I hesitated, but just for a moment. No, I had to do this. This powerful, beautiful river had gotten into my blood; to touch its actual source had almost become a symbol of my reason for coming to Gangotri. You don't

---

* I later read that some scientists question whether the river actually begins at this glacier or starts higher up and merely runs under the glacier. Either way, the ancient sages have already revealed that the true source of the Ganga is indeed higher. It starts, they say, in heaven.

climb a mountain to stick the flag 100 feet from the top. You go all the way and put it down at the highest point. Besides, the ice was all falling from the glacier on the other side of the river, which was exposed to occasional sun. The spot where I was headed was perennially shaded and covered with accumulated dust and dirt. I deduced from this that no ice had fallen from the part of the glacier where I was headed for some time.

Climbing over boulders of rock and ice, finally I reached the glacier. It loomed above me ominously, an unpredictable behemoth of inconceivable mass. Fearful that at any moment it might awaken to crush me, I tapped it—very lightly, with just two fingers—and ran back to safety. Scott greeted me with a smile as he shook his head in disbelief over my foolhardy risk-taking. We celebrated my conquest with a bag of potato chips.

At Gaumukh, the primary source of the Ganga. Note the piles of fallen ice at the mouth of the cave. This was a safer shot.

Now we began our long descent. I was stiff and sore and fully prepared for a very uncomfortable hike. Little did I know that I was about to face the greatest physical trial of my life.

Almost immediately it started to rain, and thick fog closed in on us. We put on cheap, yellow plastic Indian rain slicks and walked briskly, but we were soon completely soaked. I had never had knee trouble before, but as we descended, my knees began to ache. Sitting in my cold cave in full lotus posture for so many hours a day must have weakened them. I forced myself to keep going, but the pain steadily worsened. Before long, walking became agonizing torment. With each step, it literally felt like a nail was being driven into my knees.

As I dragged myself along the trail in anguish, Scott decided to break his ten-day silence by merrily singing *Onward Christian Soldiers*. He literally skipped down the mountain in song, oblivious to what I was going through. I fell far behind. Periodically, he stopped and waited for me to catch up.

After a few kilometers of this, I was in so much pain that I contemplated asking Scott to find a donkey for me to ride. They had to be available to rent from somewhere because I had seen them on the trail earlier in the day. But now it was late afternoon, and at that hour, I had no idea where to find one. I settled for writing Scott a note asking if he could carry my daypack. Looking into my face, he realized the agony I was in. He took my pack and put it on over his own. Though this lightened my load by perhaps only six or seven pounds, it brought great relief.

Soon, however, my knees adjusted to the lessened load, and the torment of walking seemed as bad as ever. Only by the greatest exercise of will to ignore the pain was I able to take even one step. Yet this I had to do, step after step after endless step. It was the worst torture I had ever in my life been forced to endure. I dreaded seeing the markers on the trail each tenth of a kilometer, telling what little progress my agony was yielding.

Finally, the rain stopped and a patch of sky cleared. A golden-red sun was fast setting behind the mountains at the low end of the valley. We had 9 kilometers to go. To be caught on that trail for the night, in cold, wet clothes, would be an invitation to hypothermia.

Now and then we passed porters carrying supplies up the trail from Gangotri to the tea stalls further up. These wiry little fellows, no bigger than myself (5'6"), carried unbelievable loads. One had multiple wooden cases of soda pop tied to his stooped back—perhaps a hundred or so full bottles. Another had two, five-gallon containers of kerosene hanging from a pole across his shoulders.

Watching those porters, I felt I was witnessing super-human strength with my own eyes. Surely those humble little guys had, in a past life, actually been highly evolved yogis endowed with yogic powers. They must have abused their powers and now, with the remnant of their spiritual puissance, had to carry these loads up and down the mountain as penance. Or so I speculated. In any case, shamed by their inconceivable feats, I could not bring myself to ask one to find a donkey for me. I plodded on in agony.

Twilight was fast fading into night, and Scott had to wait longer and longer for me. Then, at one point, as I caught up with him, he walked up to me, grabbed me by my shoulders, and looked me straight in the eyes.

"Ajayan, you've been meditating all these years. You've got shakti. You can use your yogic power to do this. We can't be caught up here in the dark. Come on, guy!" With this, he gave me a sturdy whack on the back.

Surprisingly, this little pep talk actually helped. In fact, it instigated an experience of vivid witnessing.

Intense physical pain was such a rarity in my life that I had allowed myself to completely identify with my tortured knees. I had been praying to Amma, to Jesus, to Mary, to my favorite saints, to Shiva—to anybody—but my knees had still been killing me. As long as I had identified with the pain, no discernible divine help had been forthcoming. From this point on, however, I repeatedly reminded myself that I was not my body. I was consciousness, the Self, Brahman. Immediately, I began to feel above and beyond my body's agony, witnessing myself walking. The pain was just as intense as ever, but I was separate from it and could continue walking, nearly keeping up with Scott.

After a kilometer or so of this, however, the torture again became so intense that even though witnessing it, I felt I couldn't continue. My body was collapsing with or without my identification. I also felt certain I must be permanently damaging my knees. Yet it was nearly dark, and there was really no choice; being stuck on that mountain could mean death. I simply had to go on.

Again, Scott's pep talk came to me. Surely, in all those years of meditation, I had gained the power necessary to see me through this crisis. So now I tried another tactic, telling myself, "This pain doesn't exist, neither does this body. It is an illusion; it is only Brahman, pure bliss. I am Brahman. All this is Brahman."

As I repeatedly thought along these lines, something remarkable happened: The pain actually began turning into bliss. At first it was mostly pain and a little bliss; then half pain, half bliss; then exclusively a sweet and delicious bliss. Not only did the pain entirely dissolve, but I felt a tangible bubble of grace surround me, an orb of sublime silence and soft, holy, white light that extended a good five feet around me in all directions. Within that bubble of divine light and grace, walking became nearly effortless. I had never in my life felt anything like it. I quickly caught up with Scott. Passing him, I felt a wave of great love and gratitude for him.

At this point complete darkness set in, and we resorted to our flashlights to light the trail. We walked briskly and arrived in Gangotri about nine-thirty. On familiar ground and assured of being in bed soon, I relaxed and let Scott again take the lead.

We continued along the path from town and got to within a couple hundred yards of our caves when suddenly my flashlight died. A few seconds later, Scott's flashlight died. We stood there in the forest, in complete darkness, dumbstruck at our bad fortune. How could it be that both our flashlights died simultaneously? It seemed a cruel impossibility. My batteries were weeks old. Scott had just put new batteries in his that morning. What kind of test was God giving us now? Already pushed beyond my physical capacity, were we to be stuck spending the night shivering in the cold, only minutes away from our caves?

We were in the thick of the forest, and the night was overcast; we could not even see our hands in front of our faces, much less make out the trail. I had been following Scott mindlessly and had no idea where on the trail we were. Scott didn't know the trail well enough to find the way in the dark. Taking the lead, I tried to feel my way towards a large boulder that marked where we would depart from the main trail to get to our caves. It had to be towards our right, in the direction of the river, and I felt it had to be close.

We walked like two blind men towards the river, hands held out in front of us so as not to hit a tree, shuffling our feet so as not to trip. The sound of the Ganga grew louder.

After a few minutes of shuffling in the darkness, the river's roar became deafening. We both stopped with the simultaneous realization that we were standing just a few feet from the canyon's edge—a drop of at least two hundred feet. A few shuffling steps more, and we would have fallen off.

This pushed Scott to the breaking point. "Ajayan!" he yelled. "It's time to come out of silence and get serious about finding our caves. Do you know where we are or not?"

I figured my silence had nothing to do with our problems, and I couldn't see how talking would help. Besides, I was already as serious as could be. We were both tested by fatigue, cold, hunger, and altitude. I knew we had to get back, and soon.

I felt for his arm and pulled at his sleeve so he would follow me. Based on the proximity of the canyon to the trail, I now had a hunch where we were. I veered right, and after a couple of minutes of shuffling, we came to the large boulder I had been looking for. Its black shape stood silhouetted against a starry open space in the trees.

"Oh, okay," said Scott, "so you do know where we are."

We left the main trail, and within a couple of minutes arrived at the entrance of my cave.

Outside the cave, Scott built a fire and made some hot milk. I couldn't think of eating or drinking anything. I collapsed on my cave's floor, lying on my back with my wet clothes still on. My arms and legs were spread awkwardly, but for 45 minutes I did not so much as move a finger.

What an austerity! What a pilgrimage! Never again would I complain about the pain of purification in meditation. Yet the bubble of grace was still with me, a blazing divinity shining from my heart and head. It had nothing to do with me, my ego, or my mind. I could take no credit for it. It was sheer grace, plain and simple. Was it the gift, perhaps, of having made that pilgrimage to the source of the holy Ganga? I could not say, but it seemed so.

As I lay there spread eagled, I saw something I had not seen so clearly before. Who had been striving for so many years? Who had been striving in coming to Gangotri, in spending months meditating in my cave, in walking to Gaumukh? My ego. My ego was filled with desire, albeit desire for spiritual experience and enlightenment. This desire itself thickened my consciousness and veiled my Self. It distracted me from the fact that I already AM. Yes, all this striving had filled me with Shakti, but that was largely irrelevant to my enlightenment. Who am I really? Who am I under this desire?

With that thought, my awareness seemed to shift from my head into my heart. I sank into stillness. Nothing. Openness. Peace. This is Who I already am. There is nothing to achieve or realize, nothing to desire. Anything that I can achieve can also be lost, but this I ever am. And in that moment, it felt both wonderful and simply normal, nothing special at all.

I cannot maintain a superconscious state of intensity, but I can always simply Be. I can be the Self that I already am and always will be. This is normal. This is wonderful, and nothing special. Not only can this be maintained, it already is, always . . .

I removed my wet clothes, climbed under my blankets, and slipped into the peace of sleep.

Enlightenment is not just an experience,
It is knowledge.
Enlightenment is not just knowledge;
It is the experience
Of knowledge
Dissolving the experiencer.

To my surprise, I awoke as usual several hours before dawn, my head full of soft light and shakti, as if I had meditated the entire night. As a matter of fact, I realized that I had been awake all night. Not that I was unable to sleep; I had slept deeply and had lots of dreams as well. But an inner awareness had remained throughout the night, giving me the sense of complete wakefulness. After the exertion of the previous day, I had expected to sleep in. I certainly hadn't anticipated witnessing sleep and feeling such bliss and spiritual energy upon waking.

I began my early morning meditation, or more accurately, I sat. There was no meditation. Within me and without was just pervasive silence, a solid wall of stillness, peace, and shakti. My mind was devoid of movement of thought, effortlessly held in wholeness—vast, empty, yet sublime beyond description.

Nothing exists. Not this cave, not the world, not I. There is no me, no sore knees, no body, no ignorance, no enlightenment, no striving. Only This.

With the morning light, I crawled out of bed—and continued crawling on all fours out of the cave. I didn't dare stand. My knees ached ominously.

It was a rainy day, perfect for leaving. We had planned to stay one more day to pack and rest before starting our long journey to Kerala, but now the impulse to go was strong in me. It was time.

As I stood outside in the rain, I felt a moment of sadness. Here I was, leaving Gangotri, and I was not enlightened. How I had wished to merge in God and be a shining example of my spiritual ideals, an embodiment of love and compassion. Was I destined to die still seeking, never realizing my dream?

No sooner had this thought come when a revelation opened my heart and mind:

The thought I am not realized *is just that, a mere thought. Wishing for what I have not realized is just an idea; it is no more than a dream. That is all that stands in my way. I am . . .*

My happiness and fulfillment depend on nothing external at all. Success depends upon no specific achievement. I am happy and fulfilled simply because that is my nature. My life is perfect, just as it is. It has unfolded perfectly to be exactly what it should be. Knowing this fully, all the time, is to have realized everything. In this knowing, my mind is in harmony with what is, with Being.

Others may look at my life and see imperfection. I respect their perception and can learn from it, but it is their perception, from their level of consciousness, which cannot know the perfection of another's life until they've realized the perfection of their own—and then they will see only perfection everywhere.

I thought of the prayer from the Upanishads:

Om
Purnamadah Purnamidam
Purnaat Purnamudachyate
Purnasya Purnamaadaya
Purnameva Vashishyate
Om Shanti Shanti Shantihi

That is fullness (or perfect). This is fullness (or perfect).
What comes from fullness is fullness.
What remains after fullness is taken from fullness
is yet fullness.
Om peace, peace, peace.

Returning to my cave, I broke silence by softly chanting. I started with a prayer for the happiness of all beings, and I ended with *Purnamadah Purnamidam*. I savored the vibrations of holiness from the powerful Sanskrit syllables.

Bracing myself on my walking stick, I carefully got to my feet and hobbled down the slope, like a war-torn veteran, towards Scott's cave. He was sitting in his bed, wrapped in his shawl, his wool hat on, deep in meditation. I whispered to him my plan to leave that morning. He nodded in agreement.

After packing, we left our remaining supplies in my cave for my Italian friend. Then we started for the bus stand in town. I limped along, supporting myself by my walking stick. With my heavy backpack on, the going was slow. We arrived at the bus stand just as the bus pulled out, missing it by only ten seconds.

While waiting for the next bus, Scott sat at a tea shop for breakfast. I decided to say good-bye to Swami Krishnadas.

I hobbled over to the ashram porch where he and his buddy were camped; I found them drinking tea.

"Hari Om," I greeted them in a voice weak from observing silence.

"Hari Om," they said with broad smiles.

"I have broken silence," I said.

They nodded, smiling warmly.

"I am leaving today."

They looked concerned, but nodded again.

"I must go back to my family, to Amma's ashram."

At this, Krishnadas's face lit up. Looking at me, his big, brown eyes shining with love, he said, "Yes, go your Mataji; she give you *Sannyasa*.* Then come back and we do sadhana together."

I smiled. "You come to our ashram and see me and Amma. She's a mahatma."†

"*Your* mahatma," Krishnadas said.

We were quiet.

"Hari Om," I said finally.

"Hari Om," they returned somberly, their eyes filled with tenderness.

I slowly walked back to join Scott at the bus stand, wondering if I would ever see my dear friend, Krishnadas, again. Little did I know in that moment that though I would return to Gangotri many times, I would never again see Krishnadas, at least to this day.

As our bus began its descent, Scott and I looked across the canyon to try to spot our caves hidden in the distant trees. I thought I caught a fleeting glimpse of the boulder that was the roof of my cave. I felt a pang in my heart.

---

* A vow of formal renunciation of all things worldly and dedication to spiritual life.

† A great soul.

That cave, the forest, river, and canyon, those mountains, had all become dearest friends. What friend has ever treated my soul more kindly? How to part with a place that had shown me so much of the Divine, of the inner and outer universe? How to part with the dear people of Gangotri? The bus turned a corner, and I relaxed into my seat.

The bus was riotous with loud voices, blaring music, and a toddler's persistent crying. The air was choked with clouds of cigarette smoke. Still, I felt a deep peace. Silence was here, too, exquisitely holy, pervasive silence—the parting gift of those sacred Himalaya.

No matter where you go, you will hear these mountains whispering their songs of Being. The Himalaya are not just in Asia. They are everywhere, a part of you . . .

Acknowledgments

My deepest gratitude to:

My beloved, Keesha, my greatest support, partner, and life teacher, who daily shows me what it means to be fully human; my daughters, Sudha and Ranjini, for their love and sacrifice, both while I was away in the Himalayas and during the writing of this book; my parents for their loving encouragement; Amrita, for supporting my retreat; my teachers, especially Maharishi Mahesh Yogi and Amma, without whom I would know nothing of this spiritual science; all those sincere spiritual seekers I have met on my journey, my students, and all my dear friends in the Himalaya.

In special memory of Swami Dineshananda, for his loving friendship and guidance.

With Swami Dineshananda in 2004

Song of Me

by Swami Dineshanandaji (Avadhuta Baba)

Let the HEART and MIND be filled with HE
Adorable One, Pure Consciousness, That is ME.
In ME alone all come and go
With Blissful heart DINESHA glows.

None other than ME, exist who?
Whom I reject, welcome who?
All that shines forth, because of ME,
Slept in Bliss, what disturbs ME?

Vanished all worries of me and mine,
In this Heart, the beauty shines.
Me dresses the five costume sheaths
So-ham, So-ham, ME sings with every breath.

Can birth and death dare to touch ME?
Can evil and good have power to blot ME?
Can Maya sheaths envelope ME?
Can three gunas have strength to tie ME?
In Freedom Absolute Dinesha shines as "ME."

Narada, Sanaka, and angels sing my glory.
Birds and bees, flowers and streams, tell my story.
I am the substratum of the Universe.
On ME plays this whole Universe.

When this lion of might moves,
All the dweller's fleet into the grooves.
Eat, drink, and more miles, awake in nights;
In bliss alone I move, by my own light.

Me witnessed the "Truth" in Me as "ME."
Duality sinks by my winks; Brahman am I.
Cause and Effect play no role in ME,
Flame of Knowledge (Truth) shines as ME.

This Fakir's blissful breeze ever blew
Path of Vedas are only Lanes True.
All the knots of attachment cut asunder,
"THAT THOU ART" roars Dinesha in wonder.

"I am That I am," none other than ME,
As dream I witness all this to be.
I alone appear as multiforms of beings,
The In-dweller, Witness, Imperishable Being.

My thirst for That none understand.
Let stupid world speak as they can.
I drank Ambrosial Bliss in my own light.
Duality is unaware in that Awareness Bright.

As mighty Himalayas, I be unmoved,
Come what or not, always in blissful mood.
Friends or foes, none is there for ME.
Sings with Ganga, always in glee.

World discarded, seeing my bliss as madness,
But Ganga took Me on her lap with kindness.
Now Flute of Life sings, with love together,
I embrace all, because Dinesha have no other.
This "Song of Me" Nature sings forever,
Dinesha shines in sky; darkness comes, never.

Glossary

Advaita, Advaita Vedanta　The teaching of nonduality: all is nothing but the Self, Brahman, one infinite, homogenous wholeness of consciousness.

ahimsa　"Not hurting," that is, non-injury to others in thought, word, and deed. Ahimsa is one of the five yamas, or observances, described in Patanjali's *Yoga Sutras.* The yamas, which offer guidance to an aspirant in his or her relation with the environment, are one of the eight limbs of yoga, the systematic path to union with the Divine.

annakshetra　Place of dining where free, charitable meals are served for sadhus, beggars, and pilgrims in need.

asana　Any hatha yoga posture; also, a seat or cloth on which to sit.

Atman　The innermost, divine Self.

avadhuta　An enlightened person no longer bound by the usual social conventions.

Ayurvedic   Pertaining to Ayurveda, the "knowledge of life," India's ancient, traditional system of natural medicine.

baba   A term of respect; a spiritual master; father.

bandhas   Literally, locks. There are several bandhas, namely: mulabandha (contracting the perineum), uddiyana bandha (pulling the abdomen towards the spine), jalandhara bandha (tucking the chin to where the chest meets the throat), and mahabandha (the combination of the previous three bandhas). Bandhas have the effect of awakening and amplifying the subtle energies, and pushing prana (life-force) through the nadis (subtle channels). This expansion of prana throughout the system is a powerful aid to meditation.

Bhagavad Gita   "Song of God"; The famous dialogue between Lord Krishna and Arjuna, which took place on the verge of the great war on the battlefield of Kurukshetra. Consisting of 18 chapters, it is considered by many Hindus to contain all knowledge relevant to human spiritual growth. The *Bhagavad Gita* is contained within the world's longest epic, the *Mahabharata*.

Bhagavan   The blessed, supreme Lord; a divine, resplendent personality endowed with the six auspicious attributes of supremacy, prowess, fame, wealth, supreme knowledge, and detachment.

Brahmaloka   The highest heaven; the world of Brahma, the Creator.

Brahman   The Great; the Self; one homogeneous wholeness of pure consciousness, within which all the objects of the universe and all of time and space are insubstantial superimpositions; absolute knowledge; the knower. According to Advaita Vedanta, Brahman is the highest realization attainable.

chakra "Wheel"; chakras are centers of spiritual energy in the body, the primary ones being located along the spine and in the head. The primary centers are: **muladhara** in the region of the perineum; **sva-dhishthana** at the level of the genitals; **manipura** at the level of the navel; **anahata** at the level of the center of the chest; **visuddha** at the level of the base of the throat; **ajna** at the point between the eyebrows; **sahasrara** (technically not considered a chakra, but a primary spiritual center of consciousness nonetheless) at the crown of the head.

chapatti Unleavened, flat, wheat bread.

chinmudra A classical positioning of the fingers, often adopted for meditation, in which the tip of the fore-finger meets the thumb. The remaining three fingers are held straight. This symbolizes the state of union of the individual self (forefinger) with the universal Self (thumb), in which the three gunas (primary constitu-ents of nature or relative existence, symbolized by the remaining three fingers) or three ordinary states of consciousness (waking, sleeping, dreaming) have been transcended.

darshan Grace-filled presence of a saint or deity, con-sidered a blessing to receive.

dahl Thick, curried, bean soup (usually made of lentil or mung beans).

Dev bhumi "Land of the gods"; a name given to the region of the Himalayas in which the events described in this book took place.

dhoti A large piece of cloth wrapped around the waist to form a skirt (worn by men).

ghat A landing or wide steps on a river used for bathing.

guha Cave.

hatha yoga The science of achieving Self-realization through mastery and purification of the body. One facet of hatha yoga entails adopting various physical postures (yogasanas); this enhances health and gradually cultures the mind/body to sustain the state of union with the Divine.

hatha yogi Dedicated practitioner of hatha yoga.

japa Repetition of a mantra, usually inaudibly.

japa mala A rosary, the beads of which are used for counting repetitions of a mantra.

karma Action, as well as the fruits of action, which must be reaped by the person acting. The law of karma is: "As you sow, so shall you reap."

Kundalini Shakti Spiritual energy conceptualized as serpent power coiled in the root chakra, the muladhara. Coiled like a snake means potential energy. She is coiled around Shiva in the muladhara so tightly that in truth she is not different from Shiva, or pure spirit. She is the creative potency of Shiva, responsible for giving rise to the appearance of the universe. Awakened through intense spiritual practices, the Kundalini Shakti rises up the spine through the various centers of spiritual energy (see "chakra") to the crown of the head, opening the sahasrara, or thousand-petaled lotus, leading to intense bliss and liberation. Opening the sahasrara represents again the union of Shakti with Shiva, now in absolute consciousness, no longer simply in quiescent potentiality.

kutir Hut.

Mahabharata   The world's longest epic, by the sage, Veda Vyasa. A storehouse of spiritual wisdom and numerous legends and parables, it recounts the struggles of the righteous Pandavas against the forces of evil embodied by the Kauravas, their cousins. The famous *Bhagavad Gita* is contained within the *Mahabharata.*

mahatma   "Great soul"; an enlightened person, or at least one of expansive spiritual vision who serves a great purpose on earth.

mahavakyas   Great aphorisms. Concentrated expressions of absolute Truth, usually from the Upanishads, which the guru traditionally relates to the disciple to confirm and integrate the disciple's dawning realization of Brahman. The four classic Mahavakyas are: 1) *Prajnanam Brahma,* "Consciousness is Brahman"; 2) *Ayam Atma Brahma,* "This Self is Brahman"; 3) *Tat Tvam Asi,* "That Thou Art"; 4) *Aham Brahmasmi,* "I am Brahman."

mantra   A sacred formula consisting of Sanskrit seed syllables and/or words, the repetition of which can awaken one's spiritual energies and the divine potential within one.

mauna   Observing silence.

mauna baba   A term of respect for a sadhak or a spiritual master who observes a long-term vow of silence.

mudra   Gesture of the hands or other parts of the body that reflects subtle energy in a specific way, also creating a particular "mood" or mental attitude. These become very effective and powerful once one is attuned to prana and the flow of subtle energy. To the adept, they are great aides to living higher consciousness.

padmasana   Full lotus position, an ideal sitting posture for meditation in which the right foot is placed on the left thigh and the left foot on the right thigh (with heels against the lower abdomen), and the back held straight.

Pandu   Pandu was a king in ancient India and father (though not biologically) of the five Pandavas—Yudhishthira, Bhima, Arjuna, Nakula, and Sahadeva—the heroes of the *Mahabharata*.

Parvati   Divine consort of Lord Shiva.

Patanjali   Author of the *Yoga Sutras;* he is the foremost ancient exponent of Yoga Philosophy.

prana   Life breath; subtle vital airs operative in all bodily functions.

pranayama   Specific practices of regulating the breath, designed to enhance, strengthen, refine, and balance the functioning of prana in the body. This aids meditation and improves health and vigor. Pranayama is one of the eight limbs of yoga described by Patanjali in his *Yoga Sutras.*

prasad   Offerings consecrated by puja (religious ritual) or by the touch of a saint, which are then distributed to the faithful. To partake of prasad is considered a blessing.

puja   Religious ceremony of worship.

sadhak   One whose life is dedicated to realizing their spiritual goal.

sadhana   Spiritual practices.

sadhu   One who has renounced possessions and leads a life dedicated to realizing their spiritual goal; a religious mendicant.

Sannyasa   Initiation into complete renunciation of the world, conferring the status of Swami.

Sannyasin   One who has been initiated into Sannyasa, complete renunciation of the world; a Swami.

Shakti   Spiritual energy, which may be tangibly experienced by the sadhak within his or her own body and consciousness; the active aspect of Brahman (the eternally peaceful, silent Self), conceptualized as the divine Feminine, the Goddess.

Shiva   The Auspicious One; the Absolute; the eternally silent aspect of Brahman conceptualized as the male principle; the divine personification of the destructive principle in nature.

siddhis   Supernormal yogic powers, for example, levitation, walking on water, mind reading, invisibility, prescience, and so on. Such powers may come to a yogi naturally as he evolves towards realizing the infinite Self, or they may come to an advanced devotee through intense devotion. These powers may also be purposely developed by various means, such as specific meditative practices, austerities, certain herbs, or incantations.

Swami   One who is self-controlled, a master of themselves, and a renunciate. The status of Swami is officially granted through initiation into Sannyasa.

tapas   *Tapah* means heat or fire. Tapas is any spiritual practice performed intensely and in a spirit of asceticism. This generates subtle heat that burns away the impurities in the body, heart, and mind of the aspirant, gradually endowing him or her with radiant spiritual energy.

thali   A smorgasbord of Indian dishes.

Upanishads   Concluding segment of the Vedas, thus called *Vedanta* or "end of the Veda," dealing with ultimate Truth. Includes the teaching of Advaita or non-duality. There are 108 existing Upanishads.

yoga   "Union," of the individual self with the divine, universal Self; also, the means whereby this union is achieved.

yogasanas   The various postures of hatha yoga.

Yoga Sutras of Patanjali   One of the earliest expositions of Yoga Philosophy, (which is one of the six systems of traditional Indian Philosophy), consisting of four chapters of succinct aphorisms. Offers a comprehensive and systematic path to Self-realization.

List of References

Amritaswarupananda, Swami. *Awaken Children, Volume I.* 3rd ed. Vallickavu, Kerala, India: Mata Amritanandamayi Mission Trust, March, 1992.

Amritaswarupananda, Swami. *Mata Amritanandamayi: Life & Experiences of Devotees.* 4th ed. Vallickavu, Kerala, India: Mata Amritanandamayi Mission Trust, August, 1993.

Borys, Ajayan. *Effortless Mind: Meditate with Ease.* Novato, California: New World Library, 2013.

Brown, Raphael, ed. and trans. *The Little Flowers of St. Francis.* Garden City, New York: Hanover House, 1958.

Csikszentmihalyi, Mihaly. *Flow: The Psychology of Optimal Experience.* New York: Harper and Row, 1990.

Easwaran, Eknath. *Gandhi The Man.* 2nd ed. Petaluma, California: Blue Mountain Center of Meditation, Nilgiri Press, 1978.

Evans-Wentz, W.Y., ed. *Tibetan Yoga and Secret Doctrines.* 2nd ed. New York: Oxford University Press, 1969.

Gandhi, M.K. An Autobiography: or the Story of My Experiments with Truth. London: Penguin Group, 1982.

Hariharananda Aranya, Swami. *Yoga Philosophy of Patanjali.* Trans. P.N. Mukerji. Albany, New York: State University of New York Press, 1983.

Jones, Alexander, General Editor. *The Jerusalem Bible: Reader's Edition.* Garden City, New York: Doubleday & Company, Inc., 1968.

Lao Tsu. *Tao Te Ching.* Trans. Ch'u Ta-Kao. Mandala ed. London: Unwin Paperbacks, George Allen and Unwin (Publishers) Ltd., 1976.

Nikhilananda, Swami, trans. *Gospel of Sri Ramakrishna.* New York: Ramakrishna-Vivekananda Center, 1942.

Singh, Jaideva. *Siva Sutras: The Yoga of Supreme Identity.* Delhi, India: Motilal Banarsidass Publishers, 1979–1995.

St. John of the Cross. The Collected Works of St. John of the Cross. Trans. Kieran Kavanaugh and Otilio Rodriguez. Washington, D.C.: Washington Province of Discalced Carmelites, ICS Publications, 1973.

St. Teresa of Avila. *The Collected Works of St. Teresa of Avila, Volume II.* Trans. Kieran Kavanaugh and Otilio Rodriguez. Washington, D.C.: Washington Province of Discalced Carmelites, ICS Publications, 1979.

Vyasa. *The Mahabharata,* Volumes 1-12. Trans. Kisari Mohan Ganguli. 3rd ed. New Delhi, India: Munshiram Manohariat Publishers Pvt. Ltd., 1972–1975.

The Delegates of the Oxford University Press, and the Syndics of the Cambridge University Press, trans. *The New English Bible.* 2nd ed. New York: Cambridge University Press, 1970.

Swami Prabhavananda and Isherwood, Christopher, trans. *The Song of God: Bhagavad-Gita.* New York, New York: The New American Library, Inc., 1951

Note: Some verses quoted from the *Bhagavad Gita* were translated by the author, who is indebted to the following translations for guidance:

Sargeant, Winthrop, trans. *The Bhagavad Gita.* Albany, New York: State University of New York Press, 1994.

Sastry, Alladi Mahadeva, trans. *The Bhagavad Gita: With the Commentary of Sri Sankaracharya.* Madras, India: Samata Books, 1979.

Yogi, Maharishi Mahesh, trans. *Maharishi Mahesh Yogi on the Bhagavad-Gita: A New Translation and Commentary with Sanskrit Text, Chapters 1 to 6.* Great Britain: Penguin Books, 1969.

Resources

If you have an interest in learning meditation, or in deepening your current practice, please feel free to explore **ajayan.com**. Here is some of what you'll find:

- **Free guided meditations.** These recorded meditations offer an immediate taste of deep meditation.
- **Meditation instruction, from beginner through advanced.** This includes live classes, one-on-one in-person or via-Skype instruction, and video and audio instruction on my membership site.
- **Weekend meditation retreats.** Most of these are currently held at our Samadhi House retreat center on San Juan Island in Washington state.
- **A spiritual journey to the source of the Ganga in Gangotri, India.** I love to share this favorite place of mine, the Himalayas, with its magnificent natural beauty and ancient spiritual culture. Includes in-depth instruction in meditation techniques indigenous to the area, as well as enjoying sacred sights and nature.

- **Meditation teacher training certification.** This course thoroughly prepares you to become an instrument in enriching the lives of others by teaching deep meditation.
- *Effortless Mind: Meditate with Ease* (**New World Library, 2013**). I wrote this book to teach an introductory level of Effortless Mind Meditation to make it easily accessible to anyone.

It is difficult to focus on spiritual growth if plagued by health problems. I am happy to recommend **Dr. Keesha Ewers**, author of *Solving the Autoimmune Puzzle,* and a gifted functional medicine and Ayurvedic medicine practitioner, as well as a psychotherapist, sexologist, and energy healer. She helped me reverse my health issues, her own, and has helped thousands of others. Find out more at **drkeesha.com**.

About the Author

Ajayan Borys has instructed and guided thousands of meditation students in North America, Australia, Europe, and India, gaining wide renown as a consummate teacher.

In the early 1970s, he studied in residence under Maharishi Mahesh Yogi, founder of the Transcendental Meditation® Program, and taught the TM® technique for ten years. From 1994 to 1998, Ajayan studied with India's most widely revered living woman saint, Mata Amritanandamayi (Ammachi, the "hugging saint"), serving as the meditation teacher at her main ashram in Kerala, India. While in India, he spent time with holy men and yogis in the Himalayas of Uttaranchal—a haven for saints throughout the ages—and researched spiritual practices indigenous to that area. He also studied with the Tantric teacher, Swami Anandakapila Saraswati.

As the host of Mind Matters Radio on KKNW in Seattle, he interviews experts in the fields of psychology, science, relationships, and human potential. Ajayan is a certified Enneagram teacher, registered hypnotherapist, Reiki Master, and Vastu consultant. He is the author of three previous books, *Effortless Mind: Meditate with Ease*, (and as Henry James Borys) *The Way of Marriage: A Journal of Spiritual Growth Through Conflict, Love, and Sex*, and *The Sacred Fire: Love as a Spiritual Path*, as well as numerous articles on meditation and relationships as a spiritual path.

He leads Effortless Mind® meditation classes and retreats and leads a yearly retreat at the source of the Ganges River in the Himalayas. (For information on his classes and retreats, see **ajayan.com**.) He lives on San Juan Island in Washington state.

10211310R00157

Printed in Germany
by Amazon Distribution
GmbH, Leipzig